Aha!

Gaining insight through humor

WALTER DAYTON SALISBURY, Ph.D.

AHA! Gaining insight through humor

Copyright © 2012 Walter Dayton Salisbury, Ph.D.

ISBN: 978-1-936447-13-8

Designed and Produced by
Maine Authors Publishing
558 Main Street, Rockland, Maine 04841
www.maineauthorspublishing.com

CONTENTS

INTRODUCTION

In his book *Anatomy of an Illness*, Norman Cousins introduced the possibility that a sense of humor might help us physically as well as emotionally and psychologically.

Warning: Humor may be hazardous to your illness.

My attempt in these pages is to expand the opportunities throughout the day for exercising our own individual sense of humor in various fun and novel ways. Norman Cousins used the Three Stooges to help him through his pain, and each of us will have our own favorite.

Laurel and Hardy films and the more recent Pink Panther movies are some of my favorites. When my brother and sister and I went to see the Pink Panther movies, they knew I would embarrass them with my laughter so they sat on the other side of the theater from me. My brother is partly to blame for my collection of Laurel and Hardy 16mm sound films. I show them every chance I get, and once showed some at a retreat I gave in Delaware. I found out later that when I started the first film, many of the participants left out the back and went to town. Obviously Laurel and Hardy weren't their favorites.

Hopefully, *Anatomy of an Illness* demonstrated the physical health benefits of humor. Convinced of the value of having a sense of humor for its healing benefits, the next step is to expand that sense to all aspects of our lives through various creative experiences.

Laughter not only helps us survive, it makes life worthwhile.

Once we are convinced of the value of the sense of humor, we are more likely to spend time discovering and developing humor in our lives.

A friend escorted a group of elderly ladies to France and Italy. He went to a great deal of trouble to get rooms in a historic French castle, but they complained about how old it was. They wanted modern facilities. At their first meal, some ordered wine, but when it came, they felt they were being cheated. They wanted "imported" wine, not the local (French) wine. The real humor test came at two o'clock A.M., when one lady called him to complain about the rough toilet paper. They'd been told to bring their own. Fortunately, my friend, their escort, had a great send of humor.

Some years ago, I went to a national convention on education in Florida. For the first lecture I had signed up for, I was a few minutes late. I do not remember the topic, but I do remember the first thing I heard. It was a phrase that the speaker used—"the triactic existential of the human personality"—without any explanation or reference. With that he lost me. I wasn't ready to be impressed with that type of technical terminology. I had to stuff a handkerchief in my mouth to muffle the laughter. I guess he was referring to Freud's model of the superego, id, and ego in describing the human personality. Freud had coined his own terms in an attempt to present his theories. Alfred Adler, on the other hand, had expressed himself through common sense and everyday expressions.

In order to explore what comprises a sense of humor and examine what makes us laugh, I'm using principles from Adlerian psychology, based on the works of Alfred Adler (1870–1937). He was a contemporary of Freud and Jung and others in Vienna at the beginning of the twentieth century. The North American Society of Adlerian Psychology lists the following principles of of personality:

- People are social beings. They need to belong and to contribute.
- People are whole beings; all aspects of life are interrelated.
- Work, friendship, and intimacy are lifelong tasks.
- Every person is equally deserving of dignity and respect.
- All behavior has a purpose.
- Positive change comes from encouragement which focuses on strengths.
- Children make meaning of their early experiences and act within this framework throughout their lives.
- Personal freedom exists together with social responsibility.

The psychologist William Glasser, author of Reality Psychology, once gave a talk at the University of Houston on success and failure in the classroom. For him, the sense of belonging was essential to success. If students feel left out, they have a higher risk of failing, so it makes sense to involve everyone in the learning experience and not establish walls of exclusion.

I was delayed for one year before starting first grade. I wanted to go to school to learn how to read, especially *Uncle Wiggly*, like my playmates. But my birthday was in the middle of September and I had to wait. Evidently, when I did get to school, I was bursting with excitement and energy. That's my suspicion, anyway, because the nun teaching first grade taught me how to spell my first word: "pest." She put it on the blackboard and said, "That's you." Of course, a few days earlier I had told her that I had to go to the bathroom. She told me to wait. I couldn't. I didn't. Perhaps she remembered that incident and lost her sense of humor with me.

Just recently, that label came back to haunt me. A resident in the apartment complex was moving, and I went by to see if I could help. I must have been in the way of the movers, as I was called "a pain in the a--." Things never seem to change.

"Laugh and the world laughs with you. Cry and you cry alone. Laugh alone and they lock you up!" —Steve Kissell

CHAPTER ONE

The Sense of Humor: The Sixth Sense

!|,!||!

We often hear couples comment that what they like about their spouse is his or her sense of humor. One can only guess what that means for each person. Perhaps it is the ability to see the humorous side of things, along with a pleasant and positive personality.

A friend told me he works very hard at not losing his sense of humor, because the next thing to go would be his interest in sex. This was B.C., or Before Cialis. Some people seem to have a natural sense of humor, while the rest of us have to work at it.

As a child I remember how disappointed I was in one local shop-keeper that I saw as a fun person. I kept waiting with a smile on my face for something, anything. But nothing happened. I believed he had a sense of humor. He just didn't exercise it when I was around.

Here is my working definition of a sense of humor: A sense of humor is a positive attitudinal frame of mind that encourages us and others. It provides us with insights arrived at through our evaluation of perceived opposites, resulting in an "aha!" moment of comprehension.

Those "aha" moments are occasions of truth for us, revelations about ourselves and others. We are awakened to the hidden purposefulness of our actions and our lives.

Rudolph Dreikurs taught a psychological technique called "spitting in their soup," which would reveal the hidden purpose behind an individual's problem behavior. Dreikurs would often get from the person a visible look of sudden comprehension about their behavior. A nuisance child like me might be after attention. An arguing child might be after power. A destructive child might be out to hurt others the way he feels they have hurt him. A child that has given up and gone into a shell might want us to give up on him, too. A risk-taking teen may be after adventure and/or may simply be bored. Once we see what we have been doing and what the underlying purpose of our behavior has been, we are less likely to repeat it. If we do repeat it, we will not get the same satisfaction we once did.

When I was doing family counseling demonstrations, parents often told me that they wanted my help in making their children do what they wanted them to do—when, where, and how they wanted it done. They wanted the child to change, and they didn't like it when I told them they already had the power to change what they didn't like. All they had to do was change their own behavior and themselves. They already controlled the atmosphere of the home. I remember one family where the father complained about his son leaving his toys everywhere. He wanted me to make him neater. When I met with the son, he asked me to do him a favor. He said, "You know, I feel like a librarian. Every time Dad goes on a trip, he brings back toys for me. Some of them have many parts. I can't keep up with all of that." I suggested that the parents store most of the toys for him, then let him pick a few to play with and put them back when he wanted to exchange for some different ones.

"Aha!" Now we know what's really going on and can do something about it. There's hope and an opportunity for the family to enjoy each other by benefiting from a good sense of humor and a good laugh about the situation.

Having a sense of humor suggests a way of thinking about life. Gaining insights into what's going on in our lives is like being a detective. Our lives are made up of many parts and pieces like a jigsaw puzzle. In order to see the big picture, we need to assemble everything into a composite picture. Only when we get a sneak peek at what is emerging can we evaluate where we're heading and how we can get there.

Some time ago, I asked a long-married couple how they managed to stay together peacefully. They said that on the days they didn't work on their marriage, they had trouble. For them, it was a daily way of life, loving each other and communicating honestly. And a sense of humor always helped.

So much of our lives is habit and routine. It's difficult to change even a small item. But change is possible, with great effort. Something as small and as expensive as a cigarette is a major challenge. Alcohol, even food, can become addictive. We are more likely to defeat ourselves if we do not have a sense of humor that keeps us balanced and honest with ourselves and others.

It's also difficult to accept good and positive comments about ourselves from others. We feel very awkward and embarrassed. Actually, we don't believe the positive comments made about us could be true. Here's an example:

I did an encouragement exercise I called "canonization" with some teens. They took turns sitting in the center of the circle. Everyone was to say something good and positive about that person. It was to be something they believed and meant, so the assumption was that they were speaking the truth. The person in the middle was also to assume that they spoke the truth and was to say "Thank you." But if they felt uncomfortable about what was said, they could add, "Yes, but…"

Most of the kids felt uncomfortable being "canonized" as a good and worthwhile person. Nevertheless, they got some positive feedback and had some fun in the exchanges. It can be difficult to tell people what we like about them, even with permission, whereas on occasion we don't hesitate to tell them what we don't like about them, especially without permission.

The sense of humor needs material to work with, for example, recognizing options as well as perceived opposites. Where there is tension, we can use that as an opportunity for a new choice, a hope. With the sense of humor we can change an either/or choice into one that is both/and.

Are you sleeping or praying?
I'm praying for sleep.

Is it work or play with you?
I work at play,

I play at work.

Do you support marriage or just living together?
Both, living together as married.

Seven days without laughter makes one weak. (Joel Goodman)

We don't laugh because we're happy; we're happy because we laugh.
(William James)

The sense of humor is a binding force for all of our five senses. When we experience something funny and enjoy it, our sense of humor has united all the elements into a strong and dramatic image. It's not just a man slipping on a banana peel, it's a yellow banana skin that has a slippery surface. It's not just any man, it's a distinguished man who voices at least an "ouch." Practitioners of practical jokes hope that the "victim" has a good sense of humor, otherwise the person will be angry, or at least annoyed and vocal.

The sense of humor effectively provides a sixth sense (not ESP) that brings aspects of the event into sharp focus by adding color, sound, touch, sight, smell and taste. Thus, the event becomes more vivid and enjoyable, like a 3-D movie. For a man to fall in the dark on a banana peel may not provide the same amusement, unless there is an unusual sound emitted by the man in falling. A safer practical joke can be accomplished by painting a realistic 3-D–looking brick on the sidewalk. If it looks real enough, people will step over it, stumble to avoid it, or bend to pick it up.

Touch is one of our senses that we often fail to appreciate. I designed an exercise based on touch to explore our ability to identify an object as one's own among other like objects. I used lemons (hands could be used but it's less fun).

It's best when a group of about six to eight people can sit in a circle on the floor. This works well with college students who are still agile and playful. They are requested to be silent during the exercise, giving no verbal clues.

First, they need to be convinced that each lemon is unique and that they can identify one from another. A pile of lemons, one for each participant, is placed in the middle of the group. Members are asked to pick one up and get to know it. After a few minutes, they are asked if they could identify theirs among all the others. Once they reassure themselves that they can do so, I have them drop all the lemons in a bag.

Again in silence, but with their eyes open, they are asked to help one another find their own lemons. Usually, everyone can do this. Whatever happens, it can be a topic for discussion later—for example, if one person holds onto a lemon that was not theirs or someone used their fingernails and scar the lemon, etc.

The second phase of the exercise is done in silence and in the dark. The group is still in a circle on the floor and the lemons are dumped in the middle. The members are asked to help each other find their own unique lemons. Most find their own lemon, if the group cooperates. Whatever happens, there are plenty of opportunities to talk afterward about friendships, identity, uniqueness, freedom to be our own person, the value of bumps and warts, etc. Mostly it provides a fun and safe introduction to a serious discussion about personal identity and respect for others, personal boundaries, and so on. Many are surprised that they can actually identify their lemon in the dark simply by touch. We are so dependent on sight that we miss the integration of all of our senses perceiving our world and that of others.

Our faculty of **sight** can give us a shock when we are not ready for what we see. I remember a sight in a resort town that disoriented me while driving. A rather large lady in a rainbow-colored mini-bikini was trying to cross the street. My eyes were on overload. I jammed on the brakes to let her get out of sight. I never paid attention to her face. I could not identify her again, especially if she was properly dressed. It would be a case of, "I don't recognize you with your clothes on, thankfully."

Taste helps me recall certain special events. A very thoughtful lady made some dandelion wine and invited me to taste it. To be polite, I said it was interesting: bitter, but manageable. A few days later, she baked a chocolate cake. It was delicious. I told her how much I appreciated her cake. A week later she invited me in for another piece of cake—with a glass of dandelion wine. The two did not go together. I smiled at my discomfort and got it down. A negative taste plus a positive taste still comes out negative for me. The fun and positive part for me was my discomfort at trying to show appreciation for the lady's thoughtfulness. There must be a simpler way, but would it be as amusing?

A funny video I saw shows a boy emptying the Brussels sprouts from his plate and dropping them to his long-suffering dog under the table. The dog, bombarded and surrounded by Brussels sprouts, stands up and leaves disgusted. Unless you have struggled to eat Brussels sprouts and deal with the taste (and the smell), you cannot fully empathize with the disappointed dog.

An incident in Florence involved **sight, sound, touch,** and **hearing**. My friend Jacques was wearing his fanny pack in front, where he could see it. Suddenly we were surrounded by about ten small boys who proceeded to put an opened magazine over his pack. The magazine effectively blocked our view of the pack and what they were doing. Jacques started telling me about an article he'd read warning about pickpockets who do the same thing to distract you while they empty your pack or pocketbook. When I tried to point out that we had a live demonstration, he kept on lecturing about the perils of pickpockets. I finally had to grab the magazine and push the kids away to stop them. One of them had already unzipped his pack and his hand was just entering it. That little gang was very good at what they did—but they hadn't succeeded this time.

We were typical tourists, easily distracted and fooled by "innocent" children. The incident provided a good laugh about our "sucker" status. Just when we were beginning to feel sophisticated and knowledgeable about what was happening around us, little children woke us up. We realized with humility that we would be no match for professional pickpockets. We couldn't even deal with the beginners.

The sense of humor helps us see all sides and gives us an opportunity to construct a new point of view. In so doing, we gain options. We have *more* choices, not fewer.

I was invited by some retired executive secretaries in Houston to a luncheon at a large department store. There was a special that day on lobster meals, and the ladies wanted me to show them how to eat lobster, since I'm from Maine. I noticed there was only the usual knife, spoon, and fork at the place settings, but no tools to help cut or break the shell of a lobster. The lobsters came out and were placed in front of us and the waiters disappeared. The lobsters were not cut or cracked. I had nothing to work with except my hands.

While I was waiting for a waiter to return, I thought I'd see if the crustacean was soft-shelled and could be opened manually. The ladies were not dressed for a wrestling match with a lobster, and when I picked mine up off the plate, I sensed discomfort about eating lobster that way. When it slipped out of my hands and landed on the floor, there was a gasp. I had lost credibility as a lobster eater, and finally the waiters came with tools for breaking the shells and getting the meat out. Fortunately, the awkward moment provided comic relief and laughter and a willingness on the part of the ladies to do battle with a new food delicacy. My misfortune was fortunate for the success of their outing. We had added the seasoning of humor to our meal.

On a trip to Belize, we landed on what looked like a small parking lot out on a cay. My friend Jacques got out first. He was upset and complaining to the attendant that there was no taxi waiting for us, as our hotel was reportedly about a mile from the airstrip. The poor attendant was confused by his request. Finally, he pointed to some palm trees about fifty feet away and told us that our hotel was behind the trees. (Perhaps he thought Jacques wanted a sedan chair to carry him to the hotel.) Jacques had wanted air conditioning and there was only one hotel on the island that had it—and we were looking at it. It made for a funny moment once we knew where we were going and how close the plane had come to the entrance.

In summary:
- A sense of humor allows for the incorporation of opposites into a balanced approach to life.
- The sense of humor helps us catch our balance when we trip on unexpected results on the journey of life.
- The sense of humor demands a nimble balancing of contradictory outcomes into a united approach to life.
- The sense of humor can produce a surprise outcome when resolving opposing forces in our life and may introduce a new way of living and doing.

- The sense of humor stretches us in order to avoid what may seem like an unavoidable bad ending.
- The sense of humor makes us determined to see new possibilities and options where there may not seem to be any.
- One's sense of humor is proportionate to one's degree of spontaneity, creativity, and maturity.
- The sense of humor is not sarcastic. It does not use put-downs. Instead it encourages us with constructive and uplifting observations for positive actions and contributions.
- The sense of humor often means we expect one thing and we get another.
- The sense of humor requires:
  - Quick thinking
  - The ability to see and appreciate different points of view
  - The insight to grasp what others may be experiencing as well as what we are experiencing
  - A depth of perception that provides a mature point of view and emotional stability for ourselves
  - A figurative and metaphorical level of understanding, not just a literal grasp of meaning

We need a sense of humor:
- When we think we are completely prepared and suddenly all is turned upside down.
- When we thought everyone understood perfectly and clearly doesn't.
- When we are all dressed up and discover too late that what we are wearing is completely inappropriate and stupid-looking.
- When we are cooking an expensive meal of filet mignon steaks and our guests announce they are vegetarians.
- When we use a doorknob to pull a tooth and the door knob comes off and hits us in the head.
- When our faithful dog and companion lifts his leg on us.
- When our friends forget our name when introducing us.
- When the stock market is no longer a challenge in higher mathematics.

CHAPTER TWO

Theories of Humor

!|ː!|!!

Robin Williams played the title role in a movie based on the true story of Patch Adams, a doctor who sees humor as the best curative medicine. He was treating patients free of charge in his own residence at the time I met him.

A local mental hospital was providing continuing education credits for therapists, and the workshop presenter was Patch Adams, M.D. His topic was the use of humor in treatment. My mentor, Dr. Hal McAbee, asked me to say hello to Patch for him, so I asked how I would recognize him. Hal simply said, "Oh, you'll have no trouble with that."

Indeed, Patch Adams came dressed as a clown. He had the mandatory red nose. His clown shoes were a gift from his trip to Russia. He had an assistant, a fully costumed jester. Between the two of them there was bedlam.

The closest we came to discussing any serious subjects was when he announced, "We will now cover the theories of humor." With that he broke into laughter and silliness. These were the most enjoyable continuing education credits I've ever earned, so, I'm going to tread very lightly over the theories of humor.

The theories of humor attempt to deal with what makes us laugh and what the purpose of humor is in our lives. The following are some of the major theories of humor:

- Biological, Evolutionary, and Instinctive Theories
- The Superiority Theory
- The Incongruity Theory
- The Ambivalence Theory
- The Release and Relief Theory
- Freud's Psychoanalytical Theory
- The Surprise Theory
- The Configuration Theory
- The Paradoxical Theory

Biological, Evolutionary, and Instinctive Theories of Humor

This theory stresses the biological purposes. Humor is viewed as a function of the nervous system and serves as an adaptive mechanism. Some have described humor as "internal jogging," which oxygenates the blood, facilitates digestion, releases endorphins, maximizes memory capacity, restores homeostasis, and stabilizes blood pressure. In general, humor produces a physical feeling of well-being.

Norman Cousins popularized this application of humor with his use of it to recover from a life-threatening illness. Some hospitals now provide a humor room and/or humorous material.

Lacking in this theory of humor are the cognitive and emotional components. It makes an oversimplified assumption that a healthy body will automatically result in a healthy mind. Its focus is too exclusively on the adaptive qualities of humor for physical well-being and survival. It neglects the attitudinal framework that is established when the individual is able to link cognitive processing with moods and emotional responses.

The sense of humor requires humor to be a multifaceted and holistic conjunctive (positive) emotion with physiological, cognitive, and emotional aspects.

The Superiority Theory of Humor

This school of thought focuses on feelings. It stresses power over others with the resulting scorn and contempt for them. The feelings of superiority and triumph come from a favorable comparison of self with others. In this comparison others are regarded as uglier, less intelligent, weaker, clumsier, etc. The favorite form of humor is derision.

Aristotle saw a good use for mockery to correct evildoers. Some of my summers were spent working at a camp for poor boys from the New York area, but one youngster arrived in a limousine. The city of New York had provided his transportation. He had been arrested for holding up the son of the Chief of Police. At camp, he suffered two weeks of ridicule for what he had done: "You held up the son of the Chief of Police? How dumb!"

It's difficult not to mock others, especially when they seem to deserve it. This approach is limited to a disjunctive (negative) use of humor.

The use of put-downs does not guarantee victory. When you elevate yourself at the expense of others, you're playing a game of "King of the Mountain." In that game, as soon as someone ascends to the top of the rock, the rest try to knock him down. Winning in a power struggle is illusory.

The purpose of humor needs be examined. Do we use humor for closeness or distance, for division or unity, to hurt or to heal, for mutual respect or for our own aggrandizement?

The Incongruity Theory of Humor

The focus here is on the intellectual aspects of humor. The consideration of emotions and feelings belongs more appropriately with the Ambivalent Theory.

When things seem inappropriate, out of place, disjointed, or improperly paired, the ideas or things may seem incongruous with what we expect. That's when we can contrast a thing as it is, or ought to be, with a thing as it ought *not* to be, but is. The absurdity or illogicality gives us pleasure in the bizarre concept. The mind fights for congruity when the ridiculous seems logical: the greater the discrepancy from expectations, the greater the amusement.

When we went to Venice we expected our travel agent had booked us into one of the finer hotels right on the canal. We ended up in a small, hidden-away hotel off the canal. Our room was long and so narrow I could place the palms of my hands on opposite walls. We had a sink at the far end. The beds were end to end. The toilet was on one floor, the shower on another. We found it hilarious. Thanks be to God, we had good weather and were motivated to spend our time outside the room sightseeing.

Bisociation is a term used by Arthur Koestler to describe the connecting of two frames of reference in a new and unusual way. For him it is the source of development in science and humor. Laughter arises when two or more inconsistent or unsuitable circumstances are united into a new and more complex assemblage.

When I first went to Houston, I belonged to the YMCA because I wanted to use the pool. When I joined, it was only for men, and for hygienic reasons we were required to go nude. I got busy at work and hadn't gone to swim for several months. I had no idea the policy had changed. I showered and started for the pool disrobed . Fortunately, one of the members stopped me with one foot out the door. I only heard a few gasps instead of screams.

The perception of contrast is important. When there is descending incongruity, greater to smaller, laughter can result. But when there is ascending incongruity, smaller to greater, when what is insignificant develops unexpectedly into something important, wonder is more likely.

Humor results also when there is an abrupt transfer in our train of thought to different rules or logic that cannot be quickly followed, as in this story:

A distinguished elderly lady ordered a glass of vodka and a short glass of water. The waiter, thinking he would be helpful, offered a correction. He suggested that what she really wanted was a short glass of vodka and a glass of water. The lady firmly confirmed her order saying, "I can hold my liquor. I cannot hold my water."

The Ambivalence Theory of Humor

This is an addendum, in a sense, to the Incongruity Theory of Humor. In the Incongruity Theory, contradictory ideas or perceptions that are experienced simultaneously by the individual result in laughter. In the Ambivalence Theory, the emphasis is on two or more feelings or emotions experienced simultaneously. This experience ends in sudden laughter when the contradictory moods are realized.

I once attended the funeral of a young man who had drowned at his high school graduation outing. It was a very sad event. I was afraid I might start crying, as I knew him and his family. The young man was in his graduation robe in the casket. His classmates were there. I was invited by the pastor to sit in the sanctuary with him and some other clergy. Unfortunately, there was a very active and outspoken deacon in the church, as I soon found out.

The pastor started his sermon about death and young people by saying, "Once again we are here for a very sad occasion."

The deacon commented, "Here he goes again talking about death. He doesn't do it very well, though he's had enough practice."

I wasn't ready for this duet. I got my handkerchief into my mouth just in time. I had gone from weeping to laughter in seconds. I'm sure they thought I was crying when I was actually trying to keep from laughing hilariously. I was sweating from the effort to control my urge to laugh. The exchange got worse. I got weaker. Then I had the terrible thought, What if I'm asked to speak? Can I tune out the deacon and get through it? I was called upon, and I made it—just.

Tickling someone can result in a duality of incompatible feelings or emotions. There is the fear of harm from the physical aggression and the pleasure of a playful encounter. On one occasion when I was quite young, several girls started tickling me rather forcefully. I was fighting to get a breath of air and becoming afraid I wouldn't. While laughing uncontrollably, I found the experience both painful and pleasurable at the same time.

Release and Relief Theories of Humor

The functions of humor as affording relief from strain and constraint or releasing excess tension are the bases for these theories.

It's painful to try to resist sleep while driving, as well as dangerous. Trying to resist laughing during a serious situation can also be uncomfortable and perhaps cause serious misinterpretation. We've all experienced how contagious a yawn can be. Once you see someone yawn, you cannot resist yawning as well. Laughter also tends to generate laughter. Once someone starts chuckling, others catch the spark of humor and it spreads like a wildfire.

When strong feelings are created, only to be found inappropriate, there is superfluous energy. That energy is vented in laughter. A quote by Oscar Wilde shows how feelings of sympathy are built up, but then found to be wasted when the final issue is clear: "The youth of today are quite monstrous: they have absolutely no respect for dyed hair."

First, there is indignation toward the young. When this emotion is found to be out of place, there is a release of superfluous feelings in laughter. Laughter relaxes our muscles and achieves a catharsis of the nervous system.

The societal prohibitions about sex are a favorite topic of comedians. By using a taboo subject, comedians know they will get at least a nervous laugh from their audience.

A student may have angry thoughts toward a teacher. If the teacher fails in some way or looks stupid, all of that student's pent-up anger could burst out in laughter at the teacher. I had a teacher once who told the class that he was at the end of his rope with us. A student in the back of the class said in a stage whisper, "Cut the rope." I lost it. Another time the same teacher pretended to be so disgusted with us that he wanted to jump out the window. Again a stage whisper came from the back of the room, "Open the window."

This is a simpler form of the Release/Relief Theory of Humor than Freud's Psychoanalytical Theory.

Freud's Psychoanalytical Theory

Sigmund Freud wrote a book titled *Jokes and Their Relation to the Unconscious.* There are actual jokes included in the work.

But Freud was not concerned with a sense of humor. His focus was on the conservation of psychic energy. Freud's theory of humor depends on his model of personality with the id, superego, and ego. In humor, energy builds up and the censoring action of the superego, or conscience, doesn't allow its release. Laughter is a pleasant way to let go and release pent-up energy. The following quote from Freud describes the roles of these elements in his theory of humor: "The principal thing is the intention which humor fulfills, whether it concerns the subject's self or other people. Its meaning is: Look here, this is all that this seemingly dangerous world amounts to. Child's play—the very thing to jest about.

"A criminal being led to the gallows on a Monday observes, 'Well, this is a good beginning to the week.'"

There is humor in the human condition. There is a paradox in recognizing our fragile condition while believing in our immortality.

Freud's statement seems to credit the superego with strengthening the ego. The ego asserts its feeling of invulnerability. What seemed dangerous and life-threatening is now seen as child's play. Indeed, merely something to joke about, as a child would. The superego seems to function like a super guardian angel. It promises protection. It allows the ego to conclude that it's OK to run and play like a child. To use the words of

Freud: "The subject suddenly affects a catharsis of the superego, which in its turn alters the reaction of the ego."

The concept of psychic energy is key to Freud's theory of humor. In all laughter situations there is a certain amount of this psychic energy generated. When the energy summoned is not needed, the surplus is lost in laughter. Freud makes a distinction between three types of laughter and three uses of psychic energy. Freud's three types of amusement are jokes, the comic, and humor. Joking, or jesting, saves the psychic energy normally used to suppress forbidden thoughts and feelings. Comic language allows for saving energy in the expenditure of thought. And in humor, emotional energy is saved.

Freud's developmental theory involving all three types is seen in the laughter of children. They jest by making up silly combinations of sounds and words as they learn to speak. Their second accomplishment is in following the simple structure found in telling a joke with a punch line. They come of age when their silliness can serve them in dealing with sexual or aggressive situations. Freud clearly linked aggression and sex with humor. For him, jokes require a level of maturity that allows thoughts and feelings forbidden by society: what was previously suppressed can now be dealt with through humor.

For Freud, the basic pleasure in laughter is in the saving of psychic energy. The pleasure in laughter is proportionate to the degree of intensity with which feelings and thoughts had been suppressed. The joke gives the release. To quote Freud once again: "The hearer of the joke laughs with the quota of psychic energy which has become free through the lifting of the inhibitory catharsis."

Our experience does seem to show that we release energy through our laughter and feel relaxed after laughing. But Freud goes beyond this simple concept of relief and release, maintaining that the psychic energy used to inhibit feelings is energy that can be released when it is not needed.

The energy released is two-fold. It is the energy in built-up feelings as well as the energy needed to suppress those feelings. This addition is needed to balance his theory, which involves an interaction between the ego and superego. Freud allows of an economy of psychic expenditure, but he doesn't fully explain how it becomes real. How can there be energy stored when there has been no actual emotion to be discharged in laughter?

For Freud, the pleasure in **jokes** is the release of sexual and hostile feelings which have been suppressed. There is both the saving of psychic energy and the discharge of saved energy.

In the **comic**, energy is saved in understanding a funny situation. A mimetic representation of the comic in our minds suggests a comparison, for example, between the silly and wasteful efforts of a clown and our own efficient efforts in a similar situation. The difference between the exaggerated movements of the clown and our own streamlined actions is subtracted. The difference provides an understanding of the superfluous energy involved in the comic.

Again, however, there are some weaknesses in this explanation. Jack Benny was a comedian who used an economy of words and actions in his clowning. His simple hand gesture and the word "Well" did the job. His routine was far more efficient than that of most of us. Similarly, it would be absurd to make a comparison between astronomers, who think big, and watch makers, who think small. So, to conclude that superfluous energy would result from such a comparison of the two fields is ridiculous.

The pleasure in **humor** comes at the cost of a released emotion. The emotion at first seems appropriate. When the situation changes, though, the first emotion is dropped and another is substituted. Laughter in humor arises from the resulting economy in the expenditure of affect.

Perhaps a story from Mark Twain will help illustrate Freud's principle:

Mark Twain's brother was building a road. While using an explosive charge, it went off prematurely. He was blown into the sky and landed far from the site. He was docked half a day's pay for the time he was in the air and absent from his place of employment.

The emotion first generated is pity. Then we learn that pity is inappropriate; that emotion is seen as superfluous. We laugh it off and discharge it.

Many find humor in the tricky switch at the end of the joke and not in a buildup of inappropriate emotions.

Freud initiated the serious study of humor. While his reductionist approach and complex theoretical model has historical interest, it fails to provide an adequate and usable model of humor. It is certainly not holistic. It is too mechanistic and leaves out the element of freedom in humor. Without a holistic view, we examine only the separate and specific actions of the person. The person who is doing the action is not considered, nor is his or her sense of humor.

The Surprise Theory of Humor

Timing, freshness of approach and material, newness of thought and preparation, are all effects of humor. Humor can bring us a fresh and new outlook on life. It can help us break out of our routine and the mundane experiences of our life. However, when a joke becomes too familiar, it loses its novelty and becomes stale. It is no longer a creative force for the listener. Its predictability makes it boring. Without amusing sudden shifts in thinking that surprise us, there is little left to amuse or delight us. Indeed, some jokes can "slay us" and some comedians "kill them in the aisles." Others put us to sleep or make us groan with pain. The worst is the "joke" that needs to be explained.

We need an aha moment, which usually follows "ha-ha."

In Adlerian psychology, use is made of the **recognition reflex**. The client's face will indicate a sudden cognitive connection where none existed before. A sudden unaware smile or laugh reveals that the client has understood the purpose of a misbehavior or an unintended goal. The Adlerian therapist discovers and discloses the hidden purpose to the client, after which the client often feels relief that his behavior is understood and can accept himself as he is.

The Configuration Theory of Humor

This theory is based on Gestalt psychology. Here, the humor results from confusing the figure–ground relationships. At first the link between the main theme (the figure) is perceived and less distinct ideas or objects (the ground) are overlooked. The dynamics involved in the sudden reversal of the figure–ground relationship is the cause of humor. The pattern was always there, it just hadn't been seen. It's like misdirection in magic. Magic encourages us to follow a certain direction or point of view. The resulting unexpected configuration is delightfully surprising. The joke is on us, again.

Paradoxical Theory of Humor

Adlerian psychology is known for its use of humor in therapy and, in particular, the use of paradoxical intentions. Adler explained it by saying, "Everything could be something else." Adler did not challenge the power of the client and his symptom. He used their dis-ease [sic] and strength. He simply switched the goal of their symptoms to a more socially useful one. Social interest, a concern for others, is a measure used by Adlerians as a sign of mental health. For example, a patient with insomnia could use their extra time awake to think of ways to help others. The client then faces a paradoxical decision: keep the useless symptom, or give it up and get on with life's tasks. For this technique to succeed the therapist needs flexibility in counseling and a respectful and playful attitude.

Comments on the Theories of Humor

No one theory seems to explain every example of humor, but together, these and other theories can give us an appreciation of the wonder in laughter. Laughter serves us well in mind and body.

Adler's concept of purposefulness applies to the use of humor. As an emotion, the expression of humor suggests a movement in a particular direction. It may bring about physical and/or emotional and psychological changes.

The major themes of humor seem to be sex, hostility, and aggression, though anything, even sorrow and disappointment, can be the subject of humor.

Humor humanizes us. Approaching life with a healthy sense of humor allows the individual to recapture life and its experiences in a spirit of humor. This requires a new mind-set, a reframing of life and the establishing of a new perception of life through an attitudinal framework transformed by humor—in other words, a sense of humor. It may result in greater maturity and compassion in the person and can facilitate the integration of the individual into the human community. It is a means to the type of person and community Alfred Adler describes as his Utopia, a person and his community *sub specie aeternitatis*—in its essential form. (Adler used this Latin expression.)

CHAPTER THREE

Expressions of Humor

$$! \mathbf{!} \mathbf{!} \mathbf{!} \mathbf{!} \mathbf{!} \mathbf{!}$$

In 1987, Harold H. Mosak, Ph. D., authored a book titled *Ha Ha and Aha*. The book is filled with jokes and humor tailored for specific types of clients. He believes in the power of a good story, which can make a point better than explanations might. When meeting with a perfectionist or a non-risk taker, he might try some twisted adages. For example, *If at first you don't succeed, try lousing it up again.* Or, *If you can keep your head while all about you are losing theirs, brother, you don't understand the situation.*

Unfortunately, most of the jokes could not be used in pastoral counseling. For example, on page 67 he mentions the use of "Pot-shot cards." The caption for the cartoon on that page reads, *Don't get well too soon. Your suffering is an inspiration to us all.*

Obviously, familiarity with the tools of humor, or descriptors, is a prerequisite, i.e., what humorous expression would work best for us in a particular situation, etc.? To be ready requires an array of possible expressions and approaches. For some, satire might be best, for others, sarcasm, and so on. Knowledge of what is available is essential.

The following are some definitions of expressions of humor:

Amusing: that which provokes smiles, laughter, or pleasure by its entertaining qualities.

Beguile: to charm in an amusing way with possible deception.

Buffo: an opera singer, usually a bass, who plays a comic role in the opera.

Buffoon: a person who is always clowning around and trying to be funny.

Clown: usually a circus performer who entertains with antics, jokes, and tricks tending to exaggerate and distort everyday activities. Often the clown acts in an incompetent, clumsy, and boorish manner. The clown may start with a small incident and build it to huge proportions, the **purpose** being to provide a relief from anxiety. At first the clown creates tension, but then relieves the anxiety caused through his antics. **Examples**: Laurel and Hardy, Charlie Chaplin, W.C. Fields.

Comic: This person is often found in dramatic and literary expressions of what is funny in life and amusing in a thoughtful way. "The medium is the message" could apply to the comic. The method of presenting humorous content can be as much fun as the message itself. Purpose: The ludicrous, odd, crazy, non-serious situations and amusing persons can be used as the vehicle for humor. **Example:** Perhaps comic strips and cartoons that help us see the fun in a sad, depressing, or upsetting side of life are the most familiar examples.

Picture a farmer coming into a tavern smiling and buying drinks for everyone. His neighbor is surprised and asks him, "Didn't you lose your farm last week?"

The farmer answers, "Aha, but the bank just put me back on my feet. They just repossessed my truck."

Comical: whatever evokes a spontaneous and unrestrained kind of laughter.

Conundrum: a riddle whose answer contains a pun or a play on words. **Purpose:** To tease the imagination and intelligence of others with a seemingly impossible puzzle. The solution given is usually so silly and obvious that it provokes at least a chuckle, if not a groan. **Examples:**

1. What would you call a cannibal who ate his mother's sister? — An Aunt Eater!

2. Who was the most popular actor in the Bible? — Samson, *he brought down the house.*

3. Who is it that marries many a wife and yet lives a single life? — A Catholic priest.

4. What's a pig doing when he's eating? — Making a hog of himself.

Cynic: a person who has a sarcastic and sneering attitude toward others. He considers others as fools in comparison to himself.

Double entendre: a humorous statement that has a double meaning, one of which is risqué or delicate. The two meanings usually play against each other or in opposition to each other. One may be nonsexual, while the other carries a sexual meaning that is taboo. **Purpose:** To use ambiguity to hide a naughty thought or expression.

Examples:

1. An Episcopal priest wrote requesting help from his bishop. "My Lord," he wrote, "I regret to inform you of my wife's death. Can you possibly send me a substitute for the weekend?"

2. Advice to a roving husband: "Absence makes the heart wander."

Facetious: the attempt to be jocular at an inappropriate time. It could be a derogatory comment made in an attempt to be witty or humorous that is unsuccessful because it is inappropriate or in bad taste.

Farce: a form of comedy where things are stretched to the point of absurdity. It can be called humor only in the broad sense. It is extravagantly boisterous humor. Purpose: There is usually no redeeming message or lesson in farce. It is just a ridiculous excuse for fun and laughter. Plays that use "terrible" jokes to stretch and fill out a performance could be labeled farcical.

Examples:

1. A couple may comment that their marriage is so bad that it's funny. But, since it is no longer funny, they may decide to end the farce.

2. A play may be so bad it becomes laughable. But at some point the decision must be made to end the farce. To call it a play any longer would be a real joke.

Farce, (farceur, farceuse): a wag, joker, humorist.

Fool: usually a professional jester who performs in a silly and ridiculous manner. He acts as though he lacks common sense.

Funny: anything or anyone who excites laughter.

Funny bone: It can refer to a general inclination to laugh. In reality, it pertains to a place on the elbow where the ulnar nerve passes close to the surface: a sharp impact at this place causes a strange tingling sensation in the arm.

Gaff: foolish and nonsensical talk. *(gaffe: a blunder)*

Gag man: a performer who uses concise funny lines without any logical sequence and covers an amusing range of topics. **Example:**
Henry Youngman is the best-known of the gag men. The style of the following gag lines fits him: "My wife has an even disposition—miserable all the time," and "Take my wife, please."

Gallows humor: a type of humor dealing with topics that create fear and anxiety in most people. By taking a philosophical attitude toward these threatening situations, such as impending death, some emotional distance is gained. This allows the person the opportunity to deal with it. **Purpose:** To defend oneself from threatening things by laughing and showing that you are not afraid. It is a way to challenge a threat in a safe manner. It is to laugh in the face of death, to find humor in a situation so frightening it can paralyze. It offers a compensatory device to bolster morale and hope so that the tragedy of the moment can be seen as temporary and transitory in nature. **Examples:**
1. Woody Allen gives us an interesting point of view: "I'm not afraid of death; I just don't want to be there when it happens."
2. There is another variation on this type of humor called "sick humor":
"Congratulations. I hear you won a scholarship to a university, the Harvard Medical School."
"Yes, but they don't want me while I'm alive."
3. "You and your suicide attempts! Look at this gas bill!"

Gibe: a taunt, scoff or jeer.
High jinks: usually associated with boisterous fun-making and lively pranks.
Hilarity: this happens when restraints on self-control can no longer contain the sense of merriment. There is an excessively noisy display of high spirits and energy.
Humor: serious reflection on the paradoxes in human nature and in the human condition resulting in a sense of the ridiculous. The process involves an empathetic feeling of identity with the ridiculous and comical consequences of being human. Purpose: It provides an emotional survival tool. It develops the ability to see pathos in the ridiculous and the ridiculous in the serious. Humorous sayings often lead to insights.

Examples:

1. A boy and a girl were playing Adam and Eve. "Why did you hit the little girl?"

The boy answered, "Instead of tempting me with the apple, she ate it herself."

2. Cleanliness is next to godliness. Maybe in the Bible it's next to godliness, but in Washington it's next to impossible.

Humorous: when there is whimsicality in saying or doing something with gentleness and geniality that is deliberately comical or amusing.

Inane: to find something funny in the foolish, silly, or dumb, and in what is totally void of meaning and sense.

Irony: to say the opposite of what you mean; or to do something and then say, "Just kidding." This type of humor points out a distance between what is said and what is meant, between a literal statement and the intended meaning, between reality in life and just appearances. The contrast and distance are highlighted by means of the discrepancy itself. Purpose: To point out the absurdity and contradictions we experience and express, and that in a humorous way. **Examples:**

1. A sign reading, "Thimk."

2. A sign in the post office reading, "No dogs allowed, except seeing-eye dogs."

3. Life is full of ironies: the inevitable seldom happens; the unexpected often does happen.

4. A priest writing the certificate at the christening cannot remember the date. Looking at the mother of the baby he asks, "This is the twelfth, isn't it, Mrs. O'Connell?"

"Oh, no, Father. This is only the ninth I've had."

5. It's ironic: you throw something away that you've saved for years, just before you need it desperately.

Jester: a *professional* fool, such as the court jester in medieval times.

Jocose: suggests a mischievous quality in joking or jesting that almost goes to the point of facetiousness.

Jocular: suggests a happy and playful disposition in an individual who could be characterized as having a strong desire to amuse.

Joke: often a well-prepared and structured story with the all-important punch line. The quick switch at the end is part of the amusing prank or trick pulled on the listener or victim. Purpose: To throw others off balance in order to fool them and/or play a prank on them. It is an attack on those who would take things too seriously. **Examples:**

1. *"What's your girlfriend's name?"*
"I don't remember. I think it begins with M."
"Is it Marguerite? Mary? Martha?"
"No; I've thought of it. It's Emma."
2. *"Don't you know that matches are made in heaven?"*
"No, they're not. They're made in Sweden."
3. *"Do you love me?"*
"Yes, dear."
"Would you die for me?"
"No, mine is an undying love."

Joker: at times this is used in a disparaging way to describe someone who jokes inappropriately or who surprises others in an untimely and unfortunate way. One who jokes.

Joke teller: half the fun is in the telling of the story using character sketches, dialects, and whatever paints a funny verbal picture leading up to the all-important punch line.

Jollity: expressions of merriment with exuberance and great joy.

Limerick: a low-brow type of humor with the use of a rhyme in a five-line nonsense verse covering a wide range of subjects from low puns to high vulgarity. Purpose: a creative and fun challenge to express low humor in rhyme or to identify with the common person. **Examples:**

The following two examples are from G. Legmon's *The Penguin Book of Limericks.*

1. Shame:
There once was a sculptor named Phidias,
Whose statues by some were thought hideous.
He made Aphrodite
Without any nightie,
Which shocked all the ultra fastidious. (#1584)

2. Funeral:
A silly young fellow named Hyde

In a funeral procession was spied.
When asked, "Who is dead?"
He giggled and said,
"I don't know; I just came for the ride." (#1182)

In the September 2002 issue of the Smithsonian magazine, there is an article by David Stewart, *The Limerick is Furtive and Mean.* (pages 90-96) The following examples are taken from that article.

3. By Ogden Nash:
There was a young lady called Harris
That nothing could ever embarrass,
Til the bath-salts one day
In the tub where she lay
Turned out to be Plaster of Paris.(p. 90)

4. By Dixon Merritt:
A wonderful bird is the pelican,
His bill can hold more than his belican.
He can take in his beak
Food enough for a week,
But I'm damned if I see how the helican. (p. 93)

5. By O.E. Parrott from his book, *The Penguin Book of Limericks*
The limerick's birth is unclear:
Its genesis owed much to Lear.
It started as clean
But soon went obscene,
And this split haunts its later career.(p. 94)

Mimicry: doing impressions of other people, especially celebrities, and trying to imitate their mannerisms, speech patterns, and so on.

Mirth: a lightness of spirit that demonstrates a sense of gaiety, gladness, and great amusement expressed with laughter.

Paradox: a form of humor that plays with logic in order to reveal a new truth that may emerge out of what at first seems false or self-contradictory. Purpose: To perform the magic of changing what seems absurd and unbelievable into what is true and factual, what is inconsistent into what is reliable and firm. **Examples:**

1. A person who got to the top by getting to the bottom of things.
2. "You've changed since I saw you last."
"And how? For better or for worse?"
"My dear, you could only change for the better."
3. "Resist temptation."
"I would, but it may never come again."
4. Liberty cannot exist until it is declared by authority.
5. Silent screaming.

Practical joke: a trick played on someone in fun which makes the victim uncomfortable and/or embarrassed. A situation must be engineered so that another is frustrated in achieving their intended goal and may in fact meet some amusing minor misfortune. Purpose: To make someone the "goat" or victim of a planned physical joke. As a rule of thumb, it is hoped that the person who is "picked on" should be able to share the joke and laugh along. **Examples:** exploding cigars, ice cubes with flies inside, a flower or ring that squirts water (not indelible ink). The TV show *Candid Camera* provided many good examples of safe and enjoyable practical jokes.

Pun: a play on words. A form of humor that deliberately confuses two words or terms that have similar sounds but different meanings or applications. **Examples:**

1. A doctor visits a sick woman and says quietly to her husband, "She doesn't look good to me."

"You're telling me," says the husband. "She hasn't looked good to me for twenty years."

2. Did you know all the animals came on the Ark in pairs? All except the worms; they came in apples.

3. "Don't you believe in the hereafter? . . . I want a kiss."

"What's the hereafter got to do with a kiss?"

"That's what I'm here after."

4. Doctor to a male patient: "Nothing is wrong with you. All you need is a little sun and air."

Patient: "I'm sure you're right, but my wife is dead set against having any children."

Punster: one who tests his friendship with others by telling them puns.

Quip: a sarcastic remark or reply with only a hint of humor.

Raconteur: a person skilled at telling stories or anecdotes, sometimes amusing.

Repartee: the ability to reply or retort with quick and skillful wit and humor. It is a type of verbal dueling where a "kill" is made with cutting and penetrating remarks that are only slightly disguised with humor.

Ribaldry or dirty jokes: this pertains to stories that deal with sex and bodily functions and are told in a humorously earthy and coarse way. They are often told in a vulgar and burlesque style. Topics range from the erotic and indecent to the burlesque and scatological. Topics usually deal with taboo subjects. **Purpose:** To vent pent-up sexual ideas or ideas that are taboo in polite society. For some individuals, these can serve as a defense mechanism, and as such provide some relief from the anxiety that sexual matters cause them. It can be a coping device to handle threats and anxieties arising from sexual concerns and interests. **Examples:**

1. Nudists: Folks who grin and bare it.

Sadist: A person who does nice things to a masochist.

2. A joke that deals with the fear of castration and impotence:

A man who is swimming calls out in a BASS voice, "Help! Sharks! For God's sake, help!" Then in a falsetto voice: "Too late. Too late. Tool ate."

3. A joke that deals with a taboo subject:

A gay couple is watching a pretty girl go by swinging her hips; her tight blouse emphasizes her curves. One of the homosexuals, who has been following her very closely with his eyes, comments to his buddy, "You know, sometimes I'm sorry I'm not a lesbian."

4. A suggestive joke:

A young wife is caught in her dressing-gown early in the morning by an elderly painter who has just come to work for her.

"Good morning. Please come into the bedroom. I'd like to show you where my husband put his dirty hands last night."

The elderly painter responds, "If you don't mind, lady, I'm an old man and I got a hard day's work to do on the ladder. A cup of coffee will do me fine."

Riddle: this form of humor presents a mental puzzle, often in the form of a question to challenge others with a baffling problem. The perplexing and seemingly inexplicable problem is given an ingenious ending or answer. **Purpose:** To play an amusing game with enigmatic sayings or to provide an opportunity to play Sherlock Holmes and solve a difficult mystery by exercising ingenuity. The solution to the mystery presents a reward in the surprise ending that contains some element of mirth. **Examples:**

> *1. How did Jonah feel when the whale swallowed him?*
> *Down at the mouth.*
> *2. What is the difference between an elephant and a flea?*
> *An elephant can have fleas but a flea cannot have elephants.*
> *3. How can a girl keep a boy's love?*
> *By not returning it.*
> *4. What's worse than finding a worm in an apple?*
> *Finding half a worm.*

Risibility: an inclination to laughter; a tendency toward fun.

Sally: a quick, witty jab, a smart retort that is not expected. Its suddenness often catches others off balance.

Sarcasm: often a thinly veiled expression of anger and aggression that is covered over with a fragile veneer of playful teasing or jeering. It zeros in on the faults and foibles of the victim in a merciless way with harsh and bitter taunts and cutting remarks. Sarcasm can be enjoyed when it is clear that what is said is not really meant. **Purpose:** It is an oblique attack in which the hostile person hopes to gain the advantage by showing a smiling face while hiding a raised fist. **Examples:**

> *1. "One of your house guests insulted me!"*
> *"Only one?"*
> *2. A difficult actor insisted on realism. He wanted real liquor in the drinking scene. The producer finally replied, "Sure, if you let me use real poison in the murder scene."*
> *3. Two married men were discussing their wives.*
> *"My wife is an angel," said one.*
> *"You're lucky," replied the other. "Mine looks as though she'll live forever."*

Sardonic: in this form of humor, the motives of others are viewed pessimistically. It contains elements of disdain, cynicism, derision, bitterness—and that's the positive part of it. **Purpose: a** savage, sneering, scornful attack on others masked by a not-so-funny attempt at putting them down. **Examples:**

1. Common sense would prevent many divorces. It would also prevent many marriages.

2. A restaurant owner heard that a rival restaurant had burned down. "I'm sorry to hear it, but it's the first time the food's been hot in his place."

Satire: an indirect and subtle use of ridicule, sarcasm, and/or irony, especially as found in literature, to expose and attack the vices and follies in others and in society. **Purpose:** It uses humor to criticize the norms of society and examines the morals and manners in such a way that some constructive change, especially in public figures and institutions, might take place. It looks to the reform of society and individuals. It is a use of humor that permits the treatment of otherwise taboo subjects. **Examples:**

1. An eight-year-old boy came home from school, put on a dress, lipstick, makeup, and high-heeled shoes. His mother caught him and scolded him. "If I've told you once, I've told you a thousand times—don't play with your daddy's things."

2. A couple commented on never having enough money. "It's the neighbors, dear," the wife observed. "They always do something we cannot afford."

3. One honest claim for aspirin: the pills are round.

4. When you see a man open the door of his car for his wife, you can be sure that either the car or the wife is new.

Slapstick: usually a crude, low comedy type that involves some horseplay and the imitation of violent behavior. The most familiar form used by clowns consists of two pieces of wood that are clapped together to create noisy but harmless slaps.

Smart aleck (or alec): name given to a person who is cocky in attitude and offensively conceited.

Tease: to annoy and harass by persistent mocking and poking fun at another person. This type of "fooling around" can get to be very bothersome, almost like bullying.

Tickle: this involves a touch accepted in fun, though with some element of the unexpected, that causes a pleasant sensory stimulation. The touch excites surface nerves and causes a pleasant tingling resulting in laughter.

Tickled pink: this expression suggests that someone has been so excited and enlivened and so stirred to amusement and laughter that they become silly and/or their face turns red.

Tickler: one who tickles. (A good job, if you can find it.)

Titillate: this suggests a form of excitement that usually comes from tickling or some other form of pleasant physical or psychological stimulation. It often has sexual overtones.

Wag: a name given to a comical or humorous person, a wit.

Whimsy: a form of humor that is quaint, fanciful, and curious.

Wisecrack: an annoying, facetious, brash remark. The type of flippant statement a smart aleck might make.

Wit: this usually occurs during an exchange spurred on by the pressure of the moment between a "wit" and an audience. The exchange is typically spontaneous and offers a surprise twist or retort that pleases the listeners. It provides brief, sharp, clever comparisons that may be sarcastic but fun. It requires the ability to see, in an amusing way, an unexpected relationship between dissimilar things. At times the exchange can be brutal. **Purpose**: To turn the tables on a heckler; to seize the words of another and turn them against him. It provides intellectual fun by playing with clever and unusual combinations of ideas. **Examples**:

1. Kennedy's comment about his press treatment: "I'm reading more and enjoying it less."

2. Winston Churchill, when he was young and grew a mustache, his lady companion at dinner commented, "Mr. Churchill I care for neither your politics nor your mustache."

His comeback to her: "Don't distress yourself. You are not likely to come in contact with either."

Witticism: a comeback that is amusingly clever and witty.

Witty: A quick and spontaneous repartee that has an element of sarcasm, but is also witty.

Wry humor: this is characterized by distorted and perverse meanings used to achieve laughter. It is an ironic form of humor.

CHAPTER FOUR

Developing Our Sense of Humor Through the Use of Aphorisms, Haiku, Paradoxes, and Enantio Technique

!|.!||!

One of my college courses was in poetry. I was actually looking forward to trying my hand at writing it. We had a hardworking teacher, and we learned about the poets, their lives, philosophies, style, interests, etc. We covered a wide range of poems and studied them in depth. We just never wrote a poem ourselves. The class was *about* poetry, not about how to *write* poetry.

The sense of humor is not an abstraction, not just something to be studied and learned about. We need to try our hand at experiencing and expressing it. We need to incorporate it into our lives with fun. By using simple tools, we can get started doing, not just talking about the sense of humor.

The expressions of humor we covered in the previous section can also be an avenue of expression for us. However, simply telling jokes is not the same. Aphorisms, Haiku, proverbs, and paradoxes require that we reflect on our perception of nature and the world around us. It shows how we blend our sense of humor into our general attitudinal framework of thinking and way of relating to life.

Developing Wisdom for Paradoxical Living

Gurus were popular in the '60s and '70s. It was the time of dependency. We sought out the "wise" guidance of others. The Jonestown incident forcefully reminded us that not all leaders are noble, and not all cults and movements are altruistic and safe. The expressed wisdom of a particular person/leader may be very impressive, but it may not be relevant to me and to my needs in the here and now. The individual can do harm to himself, and his growth as a person, by forcing himself to live by the wisdom of others.

APHORISM

Webster's New World Dictionary defines the aphorism as a "short concise statement of a principle; a short, pointed sentence expressing a wise or clever observation or a general truth; maxim; adage."

We can use the aphorism as a means to gain insight for ourselves for paradoxical living. A distinction in definitions would help in our use of the aphorism for personal insight. For example, we can apply an operational distinction between the **wise sayings** we find in the Bible and **aphorisms**. A wise saying is like the factory-made suit. It is made to fit all persons of a given size and shape. An aphorism is tailor-made for the individual. For an aphorism to really fit the individual, there must be a great expenditure of time and effort. The reward is appreciation of the uniqueness of the individual and what fits him or her.

The Book of Proverbs and the Wisdom literature of the Bible offer wisdom for and of a specific nation and people, though much of it is relevant to most people. On the other hand, the aphorism is for and of an individual. It reflects and summarizes the life journey, story, and experiences of the individual.

CHARACTERISTICS OF THE APHORISM

1. Short, concise, pithy statement.
2. Clear and to the point.
3. A summary statement of a personal experience of the past up to the present.
4. It expresses a current insight based on past experiences.
5. It is a timely comment about the present, past, and future.
6. It represents a unique statement about the individual, but others may also gain insight for themselves by extrapolating from it.
7. It is useful to the individual, in spite of the fact it is very simple and may even seem too mundane.
8. It contains paradoxical elements and/or a possible synthesis.

Some examples are found in Walter E. O'Connell's 1979 book, *Super-Natural Highs.*

Example 1: *Someday I will attend to my own writings, and I will become wise.* (#346, p. 69)

This aphorism is brief, concise, to the point, and clear. It speaks about something learned through past experience with an understanding of what meaning it might have in the present and future. The insight is significant to Dr. O'Connell, but also says something meaningful to all of us. An important feature of this adage is the implied paradox. Dr. O'Connell tells us that he is wise enough to record his journey through life, but not wise enough to learn from his experiences and to take effective action in the here and now. He seems to describe himself like a dedicated journalist who is capable of recording events, even dangerous ones, with great clarity and detail, but is so caught up in the objective recording of events that he fails to see the subjective worth of the experience, and possible danger, to himself. He is too detached, too philosophical, too psychological. He admits to too much detachment and to too little personal involvement. What is all too real in description is unreal in his own personal life and so fails to motivate him to change. It's as though he sees an exploding volcano and records every hellish detail, but fails to appreciate his own danger. Objectivity needs to be balanced with subjectivity. There is a hope in his use of the verb "will" that suggests a determination to wake up, see reality, and take the initial baby steps necessary to change.

Example 2: *That which we fight, we refuse to take flight.* (#442, p. 87)

This has a surprise twist on the "fight or flight" theme. It addresses the temptation to get into power contests. It suggests that which we select to do battle with may reveal values we cannot let go of. We bind ourselves in a no-win contest. We cannot let go, we cannot hold on, without a power struggle. We have made something so important to us that we enslave ourselves to it. It is the fight of the addict who fights drugs or alcohol with a mighty battle. But in fact the addict needs the reassuring proximity of the drug or alcohol and cannot release it completely from his/her life. The words "Let go and let God" suggest the paradox in this aphorism. The addict must give up power and admit his/her limitations. Then there is freedom to experience a new positive relationship in, with, and through God.

Example 3: *The two most obscene four-letter words in our extroverted, control-addicted world: God's will.* (#533, p. 99)

Another temptation for the power addict is found in religion. Doing battle with earthly dragons is not enough. The power and recognition involved in fighting addictions is nothing compared to the power and glory inherent in controlling God. Some addicts become religious fanatics. God is the new field of conquest. There is an attempt to control God through rites, prayers, deeds. It is not enough to be like God. God must be made over to the image of the addict, to his/her will. It is an obscene task. The paradox lies in our human nakedness before God. Yet we feel we can see right through Him. We know what is good for us better than He does. We tell God what He intends; He doesn't tell us.

Exercise: Try writing an aphorism based on an insight gained today.

PURPOSES OF THE APHORISM

An aphorism is a quick, succinct reminder of an insight that is significant enough to change the thought pattern and behavior of an individual.

1. It serves like a traffic signal. It stops some thoughts and advances others. At times it advises exercising caution.

Example: *I am somebody, and I need to study to improve my math.*

2. It serves like a thirty-second TV commercial to get across a very important message briefly; it also motivates specific new action.

Example: *Not to act is to act.* (For procrastinators this could be a very important message.)

3. It serves as a bulletin board highlighting current messages to oneself that are important to remember in order to make changes in one's Life Style.

Example: *Worry doesn't clarify, it confuses the issue.* (A statement a chronic worrier might use to get on with the tasks of life.)

4. It is like a bumper sticker that can get a strong message across with enough humor to make it acceptable.

Examples: *Touch my tail, and see my lawyer.*
Play bumper cars somewhere else.
Don't laugh. Respect age.

REASONS FOR USING APHORISMS

Those who are mentally healthy have no need for a therapist or self-help approaches. Wrong! Mental health includes the desire to grow and to learn. There is no status quo in mental health. It is an illusion to think that we have "made it." While we still have breath, we can aspire and strive for more. What we need as an aid is a clear vision of where we are and who we have become. Youth have dreams, and their dreams need to be remembered and acted upon. Old men have visions, and their visions can clarify their goals and motivate them.

Obviously, if someone is hurting, they will want relief. But often that is all they want. The discomfort needs to be used constructively to move the individual toward change. For example, a smoker's cough may get them to stop for a day. If it is not severe enough, if the person doesn't want to deal with the cause, they may start smoking again. An opportunity has been lost for growth and a new way of life or Life Style.

Our present comfort or discomfort doesn't guarantee that we will learn and change. A new attitude or mindset requires reflection and effort. It's very hard work to change—ourselves. Others we could do over in a day. We face our true condition through our memories and the paradoxes of our life. We must uncover the self-deceptions in our life story. Then it might be possible to experience afresh some of our original dreams and aspirations.

HAIKU

The **Haiku** is a simple poetic format that can be fun and inspirational. It can be used to state aphorisms in three carefully composed lines. The third line is often a surprise and a reflection on life/death or the four seasons. As such, it is an ideal way to express the paradoxical elements and moments found in the Life Style of an individual. Some examples follow, taken from William J. Higginson's book, *The Haiku Handbook* (Higginson, 1985). The first two examples express the feelings caused by an immediate situation.

The little girl
Hangs all the ornaments
On the nearest branch. (p. 140) Cor van den Heuvel

Into the blinding sun
The funeral procession's
Glaring headlights. (p. 171) Nicholas Virgilio

The next example goes beyond a simple statement using Haiku and becomes an expression of an aphorism. It makes a wise comment and gives us personal insight.

When one wishes
To show filial piety
Parents gone. (p. 228) Anonymous

Some of my own Haiku poems follow. See if you can find one that expresses an aphorism:

No moon
Fireflies in the evergreens
Christmas in June.

Falling rain
Refreshed and cleansed
Peonies awash.

A shadow on the pond
Ripples in the water
Fish gathering.

The community of man
Like swaying, changing trees
Huddled against the storm.

Sinister gargoyles
a majestic cathedral guarded,
a sense of humor—problems voided.

The last two are attempts at using the Haiku to express maxims. The first of these presents man as social in nature and needing the support and company of others to survive. The last suggests a way to defuse a situation with humor before it becomes serious by using the image of gargoyles on a cathedral wall to ward off evil. The first three record immediate observations of events in nature. The last two are attempts to go beyond the obvious to a deeper truth.

CHARACTERISTICS OF THE HAIKU

1. The traditional Japanese Haiku usually consists of three lines:
the first line has five syllables
the second line has seven syllables
the third line has five syllables

2. The first two lines refer to a personal impression of nature and may be stated as nice and pretty. The third line should contain a surprise. It should say something that has nothing to do with the first two lines, but is related in a roundabout way. Some of my own examples follow:
A green lobster
In the cold Atlantic,
No melted butter needed.

3. The imagination is used to create an emotion, rather than state it, allowing an image(s) to create an emotion for the hearer/reader without stating explicitly what the emotion is.
A crown of grass,
Flowers showing,
Wilting on the head.

4. All five senses, i.e., smell, sight, taste, touch, and sound, should be portrayed.
The air conditioner,
A sleepy cool room,
A noisy breeze.

5. Only one or two clear images should be presented.
Glass clear and colored
Saints illuminating sinners,
Bright tall windows.

6. Do not use metaphors or similes.
7. State what is experienced in the here and now.
8. Simply be an observer of nature, not a philosopher.
9. Rhyming is not necessary.
10. Brevity and simplicity are essential to the Haiku.

Exercise: Try writing your own Haiku. Try using the Haiku to express a feeling you have about life while experiencing nature.

PARADOXES

More will be said about the paradoxical aspects of aphorisms, but an introductory comment might be helpful at this point. Dr. O'Connell gives us another example based on his distinction between dualism and paradox:

Example 4: *One of the greatest strokes of personal genius is the transformation of dualisms into paradoxes.* (#526, p. 99)

There are several theories about evil. One understanding of evil/good is based on dualism. Evil is seen as the flip side of good, the other side of the coin. Thus, we cannot have one without the other. The absence of evil is only an illusion.

Another view of good and evil considers the paradoxes in life and allows for two separate and opposite entities. The paradox suggests a dialectic paradigm involving a thesis, an anti-thesis, and a possible synthesis. There is a creative tension created between two opposites, two opposing forces, and two equally demanding truths. Out of this challenge emerges a new reality, a new relationship. It is not a static state like two sides of a coin. It is more like a tug-of-war, with dynamic strategies constantly at work as the pull of one side gets stronger or weaker. The resolution will be unique to the individual, though the elements involved are common to us all. The paradox deals with two realities, both true. The paradox allows for new creative levels of perception, rather than just facts. For example, we have achieved a major insight when we can say:

"*I am a good person who does bad things at times.*"

The ability to separate our self-worth, our basic personal value, from bad behavior is a significant insight. Yes, we can do bad things, but we are still good and, hopefully, lovable. If we do not believe in ourselves and our value, we will lack the motivation to change our behavior. A distinction is needed. As St. Paul pointed out, "*I do not do what I want to do; and what I do not want to do, I do.*"

The Enantio Technique: "*Movement does not lie.*"

Alfred Adler, Freud's contemporary, taught that movement does not lie. He suggested, "Watch their feet. Watch where they are going."

Jesus Christ himself taught the importance of movement. Jesus in fact startled his hearers by suggesting they do the opposite of what would be expected of them. He said that when the hated Romans force you to go one mile, go ten and willingly. If you are forced to give your jacket, give your shirt as well.

Dr. Rudolf Dreikurs, a follower of Adler, taught a new approach to discipline. One of the techniques he used with children was to do the unexpected. If the child was expecting a scolding, give a hug, etc. Dreikurs suggested surprising the child with the opposite of what they expect.

I survived an attempted robbery using the technique of doing the unexpected. When I was living in Washington, D.C., I was returning home on the Metro. I was exiting the escalator when several teens surrounded me. One of them put what could have been a gun into my back. Another demanded my wallet or else. With that, I threw up my hands shouting, "I don't have any cigarettes; I don't smoke; I don't believe in smoking; I'm against smoking, [etc.]" They looked at me as though I was just another crazy white man and left in a hurry. That was exactly the reaction I wanted.

This same technique and principle has application in substance abuse treatment. Therapy for substance abuse involves reversing the choices of the addict. The addict must find a new source of nourishment other than

drugs. It means saying yes to a radical new direction in life, and with new friends. The chemical high must be replaced with a natural high. A life lived on the edge filled with danger and excitement must now be tamed.

An obvious test with substance abusers is based on their behavior and movement. If the individual is still agitated, loud, seeking excitement, and manifests a getting, demanding attitude, no real change has taken place. Even with religion, which is often a substitute addiction, the individual may seek a religious form of expression that is explosive, unstructured, exciting, and loud. For a selfish, demanding, immature, controlling substance abuser to choose to practice his/her religion or faith in a quiet, humble, obedient, giving manner may indicate a strong effort to change.

Enantio Technique involves movement in the opposite direction, seeking a new way or style of living. Carl Jung suggested that each of us has a shadow world, and unless we deal with our shadow world, we will always be vulnerable. It would seem preferable to live in the light, but many seek to stay in a shadow world.

Substance abusers have chosen to solve their problems in a shadowy world. The serial killer lives in a shadow world that the rest of us would call a nightmare. They have chosen to live out their horrors.

Some choose to live in a twilight area. Even Jesus warned us how dangerous this can be, expressing strong distaste for such a deceptive Life Style.

In contrast, we have selected light, beauty, and innocence as part of our Life Style.

Each person must work to discover his or her opposite, shadow side. Acknowledging whether we stand in the light or the shadow side of our personality makes it easier to change. Then we can make a clearer and wiser choice about the new direction we need to take.

A collection of aphorisms can suggest a new direction. In a humorous vein, we might try changing some well-known sayings to get the idea. "The early bird gets the worm" could become "The worm that sleeps in gets to live another day." Let the bird do what it wants. We can do the same with our collection of aphorisms. We can try changing them to their opposites. We might find some new wisdom and insight.

One of the problems we create for ourselves is the attempt to move in two directions at the same time. This ambivalence can create deep-seated conflicts. The substance abuser, the serial killer, have chosen one direction and may have less conflict as a result. There is no conflict of interest in selecting one direction, even a mistaken goal. But radically changing our direction and Life Style can present major challenges. It's the only hope for a new and constructive life. It's the only way to recover our sense of humor.

CHAPTER FIVE

Temperaments and Personalities

!|ı!|ı!

*W*hatever is received is received according to the mode (temperament and personality) of the receiver.

Our perspective on the world leads to how we express ourselves through behavior. We act on what we *perceive*, not necessarily on what is actually out there. It's not "what you see is what you get." Rather, it's "what you get is what you are capable of seeing."

So perception shapes behavior, then behavior modifies perception. What we learn, we practice. What we practice, we become. Thus, to understand our sense of humor, we need an awareness of the interplay between our perception and our behavior.

How do we position ourselves to look at life? How can we get a new and fresh angle on it? The sense of humor offers a shifting of perspectives, allowing us to experience surprise and absurdity.

Recently I was listening to a TV anchor explaining that the State of Maine must redo its districts in order to reflect Maine's "shifty" (instead of shifting) population.

During World War II, there was a story about the effects of placing the wounded in different categories. Those who were about to die were put off to one side. Nothing more could be done for them. A second group simply needed patching up. They would be sent back to fight again. A third group had serious wounds, but would make it. This group was subject to pranks and playfulness, and told that the war was over for them: they were going home. Interestingly, this group needed only 10% of the usual dose of morphine for pain.

Humor can diminish suffering by releasing endorphin and creating euphoria. As Norman Cousins discovered, **negative** emotions (fear, anger, sadness, envy, rage, etc.) cause illness . But **positive** emotions (love, humor, joy, peace) can bring about good health.

Biofeedback works not by appealing to cognition or exhortations, but through images that **effect** the emotions. The mind *affects* the body. The body *effects* the mind.)

If we **"act as if"** we are angry and use angry movements and words, we feel the mood change within us.

I remember a shopkeeper telling about some upsetting customers and what they had done to make him so angry. Suddenly he forgot that he was talking to me about others. He started shouting at me **as if** I was to blame, **as if** I was one of them. Eventually he ordered me out of his shop with threats and curses.

In psychology there is the hope that insights will lead to behavior change and that behavior change will lead to a new perspective, new insights. With that in mind, I believe there is a value in looking at Adler's interpretation of Hippocrates' Four Temperaments. Early in his career, Adler studied the ancient Greek physician's principles, but was cautious about the use of typologies. He believed in the uniqueness of the individual. Yet he uses types to gain a general understanding of people.

A major element in Adlerian psychology for discerning the specific Life Style of an individual is the principle of movement. Thus, in order to use and appreciate the four temperaments as examples of Life Style, Adler added a description of the various degrees and expressions of activity appropriate to each. (Ansbacher, 1956, p. 169) It's interesting to note that Hippocrates felt that the chief function of the physician was to aid the natural forces of the body to heal itself of disease. Now in the twenty-first century, we are returning to that attitude.

A brief summary of the four temperaments follows along with a description of Adler's concept of activity for each of them:

Sanguine (Adler's Socially Useful Type IV)

- Finds joy in life.
- Doesn't take things too seriously.
- Doesn't worry easily.
- An optimist who sees the beautiful and pleasant side of everything.
- Experiences sadness and pleasure in an appropriate and balanced fashion.

   Constructive Activity: Walks around, or over, obstacles in his way; finds a way around trouble with composure.

After two years of intensive treatment, a psychologist says to his patient, "Now I can tell you for certain that you don't have an inferiority complex. You are just inferior." (Harold H. Mosak)

Choleric (Adler's Ruling Type I)
- Moves energetically and deliberately in a straight line.
- Aggressively confronts anything that gets in his way.
- Enjoys confrontations and demonstrations of his prowess.
- Challenging Activity: Furiously throws aside all that lies in his path.

Two mothers were comparing notes. One mother stated, "My child started to walk when he was ten months old. How old was your child when he started to walk?"

The other mother answered, "I really don't know. You see, I'm raising him, not racing him."

Melancholic (Adler's Avoiding Type III)
- Defeated anew by the memory of past failures.
- Tends to quickly give up or to proceed in a hesitating way.
- Lacks self-confidence and is pessimistic.
- Prefers the status quo or retreating; fears the new.
- Indecisive and a worrier.
- Cautious and turned in on himself.

   Hesitant Activity: Moves backward and/or inward.

A neurotic is a person who worries about things that didn't happen in the past instead of worrying about something that won't happen in the future, like normal persons. (Harold H. Mosak)

Phlegmatic (Adler's Leaning and Getting Type II)
- Acts like a stranger to life and is not impressed or moved by anything.
- Collects information but doesn't seem to follow up on it.
- Nothing in particular seems to interest him. He makes no effort to make contact with life or others.
- Seems removed from life and people.
- Was not always this way. Present behavior is a coping device, a safe-guarding process, placed like a shield between himself and the environment.

Safeguarding Activity: Stands removed from life and others, like an observer, rather than a participant.

A young boy was visiting the zoo with his father. As they were observing the lion's cage, the boy suddenly seemed worried. "What's bothering you, son?" asked the father.

"If the lion gets out of the cage right now and attacks you, what bus do I take home?"

Hippocrates' temperaments and Adler's Life Styles are not presented here for use as labels or as neat pigeonholes in which to place individuals. Rather, they are offered in the hope of finding healthy and useful traits for daily living.

Current research seems to be reexamining the possibility of a link between personality types and physical heath. Some work has been done on type A personalities and their proclivity for heart problems. Presently there is some new research that points to an even stronger link between certain personality types and specific health considerations. The results from the research on "Psychological Factors in the Prognosis, Pro-phylaxis, and Treatment of Cancer and Coronary Heart Disease" were published by Drs. Ronald Grossarth-Maticek and H.J. Eysenck, 1992; unpublished).

Four personality types emerged from their study and it is interesting that they, like Adler, describe their personality types in terms of move-ment.

First, those who are cancer-prone move toward either those persons with whom they wish to be close, or those goals that are vital to them. Inner tension results when either the person loved withdraws permanently, or the goal desired becomes unattainable. In any case, the individual remains irrevocably locked into his movement toward the unattainable. Even though there is the sad realization that all will end in failure, they are still set on a determined and unalterable course. To the same degree, they idealize the desired object and proportionately diminish their own worth. As a result, they may experience a sense of hopelessness, helplessness, and depression. Unable to disengage, the individual may also hide his feelings even from himself. Example: a marriage in which a wife loves her husband with a great love and continues to do so even though she remains unloved by her husband, and she cannot, or will not, leave the union.

It is like the moth that is inexorably drawn into the flame.

Second, those who are prone to heart problems. They need to gain a distance from disturbing objects that are unattainable or not accomplish able. Yet they continue to be linked to the object that is causing their distress. They would like to break and run, but they cannot free themselves of this permanent source of irritation, anger, helplessness, and subjugation. They may feel trapped and experience anxiety. They may have aggressive feelings toward self and others.

It is like the deer paralyzed by the headlights of an approaching car.

Third, those who experience an average survival rate. These individuals are ambivalent in their feelings toward important objects and persons. They may perceive and send inconsistent messages. They may swing between closeness and distance. To a lesser degree, they will also experience anxiety and aggression toward self and others.

It is like the chameleon that alters its appearance according to the situation and its safety.

Fourth, those who will have an elevated survival rate. These individuals are able to integrate conflicting/opposing emotions and find a useful expression of them. They can experience love and anger and express both. They can express positive regard for self and others, and have a high level of self-confidence and self-esteem. They have the ability to learn from experience. They are capable of intellectual and emotional growth and see the need for it. They possess autonomy and independence. They recognize the rights of others. They can regulate interpersonal closeness and distance, and can maintain vertical as well as horizontal relationships. They can achieve a sense of well-being for themselves. They can maintain a high level of courage and activity.

These individuals are like the butterfly whose growth evolves and emerges from one expression of life to another.

This is only an attempt at a brief description of the movement within each of the four types found in the research by Grossarth-Maticek and Eysenck.

Psychoanalyst Karen Horney investigated the basic anxiety of children and also three basic movements for coping with basic needs—moving toward people (a need for love), moving away from people (a need for independence), and moving against people (a need for power). (Horney, 1942)

Karen Horney interpreted the isolated and helpless state of the child as a cause of anxiety. Her focus is on the home, where parents can establish a secure, warm, loving, trusting, and respectful atmosphere. The individual develops various strategies to cope with his feelings of anxiety. The normal person is able to integrate all three "movements" or orientations. The neurotic lacks this sense of integration and settles on artificial and irrational solutions. The neurotic recognizes only one of these three trends and denies or represses the other two solutions. For her, conflicts are preventable. Conflict arises out of the social condition; it is not built into the nature of humans and thus is not inevitable. Karen Horney and Alfred Adler take an optimistic view of human beings, in opposition to Freud. (Terner & Pew, 1978, pp. 191–192)

Alfred Adler only trusted movement. He interpreted the individual's Life Style based on the direction of movement. (Adler, 1973) The Superior type seeks to be over others. The Dependent type leans on others. The Aginner type moves against others.

Adler observed, "Humans make their own personalities out of the raw materials of heredity and experience…The creative self gives meaning to life. It creates the goal as well as the means to the goal. The creative self is the active principle of human life and it is not unlike the older concept of soul." (Hall, et al, 1978, p. 66) Adler offers a hopeful, positive, and constructive picture of the human potential. Adler allows for the individual to be the master, not the victim, of his or her own fate.

Recent research has found that cancer patients have had the highest survival rate when psychotherapy and chemotherapy were combined to achieve a greater synergistic effect. The statistical percentages found in attempts at prophylaxis are impressive, i.e., 68% who received therapy survived compared to only 16% in the control group.

Personality and stress have a major role in disease and in therapy—even in prolonging life. Personality can predict with considerable accuracy the likelihood of a person dying of cancer or coronary heart disease.

Predictions based on physical causes, such as smoking and high cholesterol levels, were much less successful than those based on personality factors. **Personality is revealed to be approximately six times as important as physical factors.**

What can we learn from this research to help us prevent illness and achieve a healthier life? We can move in the direction of type four, but it will require altering some of our behaviors. We must consider the following directions:

1. Move toward greater autonomy.

2. Have a less repressed attitude toward our emotional expressions.

3. Adopt coping mechanisms to deal with the interpersonal stress so prominent in persons of types one and two.

This book is an effort to expand on these three points, which have been offered as guidelines for healthy living by the authors of the current research. Another longitudinal study on coping mechanisms, conducted at Harvard, found that humor, in its many forms, is one of the best positive coping devices. That study will be discussed later.

The following chapters provide suggestions on "how to do it," so in a way, this is a survival kit. It is also meant as a source of suggestions on how to have fun and enjoy life.

SOURCES, CHAPTERS ONE–FIVE

Adler, Alfred: *Superiority and Social Interest*. Ansbacher, Heinz L., and Rowena Ansbacher (Eds.). New York: The Viking Press, 1973.

Ansbacher, Heinz L., and Rowena Ansbacher. *The Individual Psychology of Alfred Adler*. New York: Harper Torchbooks, 1956.

Cousins, Norman. *Anatomy of an Illness as Perceived by the Patient*. New York: Bantam Books, 1985

Dreikurs, Rudolf. Fundamentals of Adlerian Psychology. Jamaica, W.I.: Knox Educational Services, 1962

____. *Psychodynamics, Psychotherapy, and Counseling. Chicago: Alfred Adler Institute, 1973*

Eysenck, H.J.: "Personality, cancer, and cardiovascular disease: A casual analysis." *Personality and Individual Differences*, 5, 535–557; 1985.

——. "Personality as a predictor of cancer and cardiovascular disease and the application of behaviors therapy in prophylaxis." *European Journal of Psychiatry*, 1, 29–41; 1987a.

——. "Anxiety, 'learned helplessness,' and cancer—a casual theory." *Journal of Anxiety Disorders*, 1, 87–104; 1987b.

——. "The respective importance of personality, cigarette-smoking and interaction effects for the genesis of cancer and coronary heart disease." *Personality and Individual Differences*, 9, 453–464; 1988a.

——. "Personality, stress, and cancer: Prediction and prophylaxis." *British Journal of Medical Psychology*, 61, 57–75; 1988b.

Freud, S. Jokes and their Relation to the Unconscious. (J. Strachey, Trans.).New York: W.W. Norton Company, Inc., 1963 (originally published 1905)

Grossarth-Maticek, R., and H.J. Eysenck. "Length of survival and lymphocyte percentage in women with mammary cancer as a function of psychotherapy." *Psychological Reports*, 65, 315–321; 1989.

——. "Creative Novation Behavior Therapy as a prophylactic treatment for cancer and coronary heart disease: I. Description of treatment."

Behavior Research and Therapy, 29, 1–16; 1991a.

Grossarth-Maticek, Eysenck, and H. Vetter. " Personality type, smoking habit and their interaction on predictors of cancer and coronary heart disease." *Personality and Individual Differences*, 9, 479–495; 1988.

Grossarth-Maticek, et al. "The Heidelberg Prospective Intervention Study." In W.J. Eylenbosch, N. van Larbeke, and A.M. Depooter (Eds.). *Primary Prevention of Cancer*. New York: Raven Press, 1988, pp. 199–211.

Grossarth-Maticek and Eysenck "The psychological factors in the prognosis, prophylaxis, and treatment of cancer and coronary heart disease." In *Directions in Mental Health Counseling*, Vol. 2, Lesson 2; February 1992.

Hall, Calvin S., and Gardiner Lindzen. *Theories of Personality*. New York: John Wiley & Sons, 1978.

Higginson, W.J. with Penny Harter. *The Haiku Handbook*. New York: McGraw-Hill Book, Company, 1985

Horney, Karen, M.D. *Self-Analysis*. New York: The Norton Library, 1942.

Koestler, A. *The Act of Creation*. London: Hutchinson Press, 1964.

Mosak, Harold H., Ph.D. *Ha Ha and Aha*. Muncie, Indiana, Accelerated Development, Inc., 1987.

O'Connell, W.E. *Supernatural Highs. Chicago, Illinois: North American Graphics, 1979.*

Orgler, Hertha. *Alfred Adler The Man and His Works: Triumph over the Inferiority Complex. New York:* The New American Library, Inc., Liveright Publishing Corporation, 1972

Parrott, *E.O. The Penguin Book of Limericks*. United Kingdom: Penguin Books, 1995.

Terner, Janet, and W.L. Pew. *The Courage to Be Imperfect: The Life and Work of Rudolf Dreikurs*. New York: Hawthorne Books, Inc., 1978.

Ziv, Avner, Ph.D.. *Personality and Sense of Humor*. New York: Springer Publishing Co., 1984.

Vaillant, George, M.D.. *Adaptation and Ego Mechanisms of Defense*. The Harvard Medical School Mental Health Letter. Vol. 3, Number 1, July 1986 (4-6)

CHAPTER SIX

Tasks of Life

!|؛!¦!!

The sense of humor has a major challenge in dealing with the tasks of life. Alfred Adler suggested three tasks of life, and I've expanded them to the four listed below. Corresponding to each is a required attitude for completing that particular task.

Each task has its own demands. We cannot pick and choose the ones we want to undertake; we must do them all. The very nature of **work** requires making a contribution to society. **Love** succeeds only when two persons cooperate as equals. Creativeness should flow from expressions of **religion, fun, joy,** and **humor**. If it doesn't, something is missing in the fulfillment of the task of re-creating ourselves through these kinds of experiences. The effort to include and integrate all the tasks of life requires discipline. We must exercise **self-discipline** and constriction if we are to invest adequately in all the tasks.

It may seem easier to express our sense of humor in recreation (re-creation) rather than in work. Or, we may seem to be one person when at home and another at work or at church. But the tasks require equal treatment, and each can be aided through application of our sense of humor.

Tasks of LifeRequired Attitude

Work, Vocation Willing to *CONTRIBUTE* to others
Love, Friendship Willing to *COOPERATE* with another
Fun, Joy, Humor, Religion Expressions of *CREATIVENESS*
Self-Discipline, Self-Control Exercise *CONSTRICTIVENESS*

WORK AND THE VIRTUE OF *EUTRAPELIA*

Work and play are two of the main tasks of life. Of the two, play is the one that suffers in this era of urgency. There is so much to do and so little time in which to do it. Who has the time for play? Rest is rust! Time is money!

Eutrapelia is a Greek word meaning liveliness and moderation in the use of recreation. It was first introduced by Aristotle, and it is now known simply as recreation. It was seen as the cure for weariness of mind and body caused by constant work. Too little play results in austere moroseness or boorishness in social relationships. Too *much* play may affect our social relationships and cause us to neglect the serious matters of life. St. Thomas Aquinas felt that too little play could be worse than too much.

The virtue of eutrapelia is best described as creative leisure and as such, includes religion. The Psalms tell us: "Have leisure and know that I am God." This is unobligated time, i.e., time to do as we please. We need about two hours each week in order to avoid burn-out, stress, ulcers, heart troubles, and so on.

In our Judeo-Christian tradition we have valued relaxation in everyone's life, including God. In the Book of Genesis, God the Creator rested from His works. Jesus took time for a picnic with his disciples after their first attempts at preaching. Christ's ceaseless, tireless work is often balanced with time alone in the hills or desert to pray, or just to relax. From these examples, we can learn to relax, to be still, and to be peacefully creative.

One common mistake we make is confusing the task of love with the task of work. We hear people say, "After all the hours I've spent working FOR YOU, and this is the way you show your love and appreciation!" The statement "After all I've done for you…" expresses feelings of self-pity and resentment, not love. We forget that the purpose of work is to receive remuneration and job satisfaction, not love. In fact, the harder we work, the less energy and time we have for relationships. Our work can sabotage our love.

Why do we push ourselves to work excessively?

a. We may feel a psychological imperative. We may feel driven to be perfect and to fulfill every extreme expectation. Perfectionism can crush any sense of celebration of life and distance us from love. Dependent persons may worry more about pleasing others than doing the task at hand.

b. We may feel a moral imperative: "Idle hands are the devil's workshop." We may feel that we are a better person the busier we are. By drugging ourselves with work, we can avoid seeing our real faults/values/ attitudes.

c. We may feel an emotional imperative. Desperate and starved to feel valued as a person, we may substitute work for love. Work gives us some appreciation and social involvement—better some than none. Others may overcompensate for the lack of love by replacing it with excessive work and success.

d. We may feel an autonomy imperative. Busy work can keep us from self-reflection and self-evaluation. If we keep busy enough, we may never have to stop and think about who we are and what we are about in life. The roles, and jobs, we do can give us a sense of who we are, an identity. Our works justify us to ourselves. Yet we are never just our works, we are more than that. Work can give us the illusion of self-sufficiency and value.

Some fear retirement and leisure time for a few or many of the following reasons:

- What will I do with my free time? If we have not taken time for ourselves while we were working, we have nothing to do now that we are retired. Having nothing to do is not the same as creative leisure and true play. It's easy to become a couch potato, a boorish bore.
- I am my work. The more I do, the busier I am, the more important I feel. This is the workaholic for whom success is occupation and busyness.
- I need to be in control—even of my salvation. I must do it all myself, even into eternity. My efforts alone are enough.
- My life is meaningless and empty. My work gives me purpose and value. Work distracts me from myself and other issues of life.

Quality time is what is needed as a remedy in all of these.

- We need to take time, quality time, for ourselves. If we don't take it, the compulsion to work will keep us busy with something. We will never have time for ourselves otherwise.

- We need to have the time to celebrate and enjoy life, health, freedom, and God's love for us.
- We need to share ourselves with our friends, make new ones, and renew contacts with former friends. It takes time to be friendly and loving.
- We need to be there for one another. It takes time to develop trust and loyalty. There is a beautiful story about a father trying to save his son from a burning building. His son was on the second floor standing at a smoke-filled window. He answered in response to his Father's urging to jump, "I'm afraid to jump. I can't see you, Dad." His father, standing below on the lawn, gives him the reassuring answer, "But, I can see you, son. Jump!"
- We need leisure for its own sake, not as a final reward for a job well done—we may never finish our work. We need time just to be with God and with ourselves.
- We need time for celebration. What we celebrate reflects crucial moments in our lives and what we value. We may celebrate coming of age to vote, getting a license to drive. We may remember celebrating marriage, graduation, the first baby, a special vacation. Whatever we do, if it has true meaning for us, we need to take the time to celebrate it.

Work can be enjoyable, but it is neither leisure nor play. Work satisfies some basic needs, but not all. Rest will meet the rest.

LOVE

"She loves me, she loves me not, she..." Children use flower petals to find out if they are loved or not. Adults have a more difficult task. Since all behavior is purposeful, including loving, we need to ask, "For what purpose?" Is this a Don Juan out for another conquest? Is this a power play to get something? Is it just an adventure? Is it rebellion? What is really going on in this relationship?

Love requires a dyad, two persons, and for the religious person, a triad, with God as the third party. Love requires the courage to trust and to be open. Intimacy comes at great risk. You can get loved. You can get hurt. The greater the trust and openness in love, the greater the intimacy.

But the same information that invites closeness can also be used for mischief and distance.

Love is optimistic. Love is possible and worth the effort. We have been given some signs to guide us toward a healthy and wholesome love in 1 Corinthians 13. At a NASAP Convention (North American Society of Adlerian Psychology) Heinz L. Ansbacher (Institute of Man symposium on Love and Violence, November 20, 1965) shared with me how he presented this description of love to his patients. He told me about his paper on Love and Violence. He points out that in this scripture there are eight positive and eight negative attributes assigned to love. In the following citation, the former are indicated by the superior numbers 1, 2, and 11 to 16, while the negative attributes are numbered 3 to 10.

Love is patient 1 and kind; 2 love is not jealous 3 or boastful:4 it is not arrogant5 or rude. 6 Love does not insist on its own way; 7 it is not irritable 8 or resentful;9 it does not rejoice at wrong,10 but rejoices in the right.11 Love bears all things,12 believes all things,13 hopes all things,14 endures all things.15 Love never ends.16

By this definition, love is no longer a rarefied aspiration and abstraction, but is resolved into a number of very down-to-earth, attainable interpersonal behaviors. To love is to be patient; kind; to identify with the other person's reason for joy; to be generally supporting; to be tolerant; to have trust in the other; to have confidence in the other's future; to be constant in these behaviors. On the other hand, the characteristics of the absence of love, namely to be jealous, boastful, arrogant, rude, stubborn, irritable, resentful, and malicious, are all traits of striving for personal power at the expense of others.

To appreciate how profound this definition of love is, try it!

Love and Friendship

Friendship, for Alfred Adler and William Glasser, is one of the basic tasks of life for every human being. Humans are social in nature; we need one another. Friendship is the best indicator of a person's social interest and ability to relate to others with loyalty, responsibility, truthfulness, etc. In fact, we tend to judge the character of a person by the company he or she keeps. A person who has a high regard for others will act like a fellow man and not a superman (or woman). This sense of fellowship reflects the person's solidarity and connectedness with others. This is far different from the attitude of those who "network" in order to use people to their advantage, or from the con of the substance abuser and criminal. A sign of improvement for the substance abuser is the establishing of new friendships that are not based on drug use and supply.

The example of substance abuse suggests that the type of love involved in friendship is not libidinal, but rather a function of perception. We can only be close to, and fond of, those whom we consider our fellow human beings and with whom we can be a cooperating partner in life. Posturing as a super-person does not invite closeness. It creates distance and can foster neurosis, psychosis, substance abuse, criminal behavior, and even suicide. When there is little honest concern for others, the individual gains an exaggerated view of self. If there is a failure in the I-to-you relationship, there may develop an ambivalent attitude, i.e., hesitating, regressive, detouring behavior, which distances us from others. The attempt to escape this task of life reveals inferiority feelings. Its neglect also blocks progress toward a happy and cooperative social life.

We hesitate to show what is precious to us, what giftedness we possess, to those whom we fear and distrust. Making friends does require some risks, some courage. Only to true friends whom we respect and love will we reveal our real selves and hope that they will still love and respect us. Only to a real friend do we disclose not only our great successes, but also our weaknesses and pains. Only with a trusted friend do we share our darkest moments and shadow side, as well as the times when our life is radiant with joy and happiness. We share our sighs and tears, our burdens as well as our hope, and our laughter with true friends.

But in sharing ourselves with others, there must be mutuality such that my strength is yours, your pain is mine, your laughter is mine, my obstacles are your challenges. Then it is safer to be vulnerable because we are surrounded by the creative and caring strength of a friend. Then it is safer to be open and admit our feelings because the other person knows the truth about us. It is not too risky to be honest because rightness is not the issue but rather support, encouragement, and availability. In friendship we have the opportunity to convert everything into its opposite and to make ourselves whole. Fear can be changed into courage, weakness into strength, sadness into joy.

We act in line with what we anticipate. If we fear rejection and criticism from others, we will avoid making friends. Fear of failure, rejection, and humiliation will hold us back. We may pick someone younger or weaker that we can dominate, if we fear rejection. We will make fun of others before they can ridicule us. We may not even try to make friends to avoid failing at the task. Or we may make the task even harder for ourselves by selecting individuals who are too popular, powerful, or busy. A more realistic and less ambitious attitude in making friends would be to choose someone we could easily get to know and would enjoy knowing. Aim for an attainable friendship.

The inability to identify with others isolates us and cuts us off from developing friendships. Friendship requires empathy. Friends learn to look with the eyes of the friend, to listen with their ears, and to feel with their heart.

A favorite quote of Alfred Adler was from Friedrich Schiller's poem, "Die Teilung der Erde" (literally, "The Partition of the World"). Jove, one of the ancient gods, offers earth to man, and each grabs his share—the poor man, the nobleman, the abbot, the merchant, and the king. After the partition is completed, the poet arrives and finds everything is gone. When Jove asks, "Where were you when the world was divided up?" the poet replies, "I was with you. My eye was fixed on you, my ear on the harmony of your heaven. Pardon the spirit who, intoxicated by your light, lost sight of the earth." To this Jove offers the consolation, "What to do? I have given the earth away. But you may at any time live with me in my heaven."

Jove may have been mighty in his power and fair in his creation, but the poet, in his ability to identify and empathize, gives and receives the gift of friendship.

FUN, JOY, HUMOR

As previously mentioned, the book *Ha Ha and Aha* by Dr. Harold Mosak deals with the psychology of humor. As the title suggests, insight into a problem, or a deeper understanding of our Life Style, may come to us suddenly in the midst of laughter.

The *Harvard Medical School Mental Health Letter*, Vol. 3, No. 1 (July 1986), reported on another use of humor. In an article by George Vaillant, M.D., on "Adaptation and Ego Mechanism of Defense," humor is listed as one of the positive and mature defense mechanisms. It is a major contributor to a long and healthy life. The statistics are impressive. Of men aged 55 who had consistently used humor as one of their mature defenses by the age 47, 80% were in excellent physical health, while only 20% had some physical problems. NONE were disabled or dead. But of men who had consistently used immature or neurotic defenses, 33% were in excellent physical health, 33% had some physical problems, and 33% were disabled or dead.

There are two sets of emotions, conjunctive and disjunctive. The disjunctive emotions distance us from others. The emotions of sadness, anger, envy, bitterness, loneliness, etc., experienced over a long period of time can make us ill, mentally and physically. We accept that conclusion. Only recently has the role of conjunctive emotions, such as joy, hope, playfulness, love, and good humor, been studied. Dr. Fry and Dr. Aviv and others are researching the physical benefits of laughter. Dr. Fry describes laughter as "internal jogging."

Norman Cousins's book *Anatomy of an Illness* was one of the first popular books to indicate the benefits of combining medical therapy with humor therapy. He reported that thirty minutes of laughing at *Candid Camera* and other comedy shows gave him two hours of restful sleep and eventually helped to cure him. Now some hospitals are providing "laughter rooms" for patients and staff.

Religion:

It may be surprising, even startling, to see religion in the same category as fun, joy and recreation and as a task in life.

The meaning of religion is "to bind together." A healthy expression of religion will assist us in our growth towards a union with God so that we may experience His friendship with joy. We know how valuable human friendships can be. Those relationships are on the horizontal level between equals. Our friendship with God is a vertical one. He invites us. We respond to the opportunity for growth.

In May, 1964 I introduced Doctor Martin Luther King, Jr., who spoke on the topic," Sleeping through a revolution," at Texas Southern University in Houston, Texas. He gave a challenging imagery to his audience. He suggested that a crown hovered over each of our heads placed there by God. Our challenge is to reach for that crown, to stretch and strive throughout our lives to accept what God wants to give us. To reach for glory.

Einstein evidently believed in God as the Creator, a power greater than ourselves. We experience creation, of which we are a part, as constantly in flux and recreating itself. We use the word recreation without appreciating its full meaning and purpose. We need to refresh ourselves in mind and body, to play and to have fun with others and God.

It's about time we took humor seriously. It can give us insight, understanding, health, and longevity, and improve our quality of life. There is wisdom in the familiar saying, "Laugh, and the world laughs with you; cry, and you cry alone." A sense of humor can be the oil that makes interpersonal relationships go more smoothly. A sense of humor is not just telling jokes. It is an attitude, a frame of mind. It is often the ability to see the paradoxes in life and to be amused by them.

A few years ago, Dr. Walter O'Connell, a friend who has done research in humor for over thirty years, sent me a card for Christmas. The message on the card read: "Blessed is the person who can laugh at him/herself; she/he'll never cease to be amused."

A sense of humor gives us a sense of balance and an appreciation for the ironies in life.

"He who laughs, lasts."

DISCIPLINE

Everyone is for discipline. Everyone is against child abuse. Yet there are over 40 million American adults who as children were victims of sexual abuse. The figure gets much higher when other forms of abuse are included. Ninety percent of those in prison today started as abused children. This is disturbing, but something else is even worse: about two-thirds of those who have been abused continue the cycle. The abusive "discipline" they experienced as a child is now their form of discipline as an adult.

At a workshop I attended, a member of the clergy rejected this idea. He said he had been abused as a child and wasn't physically abusing others as he had been. The suggestion was made to him that instead of using physical abuse, he might be treating others in a mean and sarcastic way. There was a strong reaction from those who knew him. His church was having trouble placing him in a congregation, as the people could endure him for only a few months. Fortunately, he gained some insight into his behavior. Without some form of intervention, abuse repeats itself.

We also pair our approach to discipline with our own personality. If we are a doer, we select an active form of discipline. If we are passive, we tend that way.

How we discipline becomes very important. Logically there are four possible approaches to discipline: active and passive, positive and negative. Reward, praise, and punishment are examples of active positive and negative methods. Pampering and pitying (excusing or giving up) are passive positive and negative techniques. These are the four P's: Praising, Punishing, Pampering, and Pitying.

Active positive/negative: Praising/Punishing
Passive positive/negative: Pampering/Pitying

One parent who attended Parents Anonymous admitted that he had never said a kind word to his son. He could admit this to us, but not to the boy. No matter how hard the boy tried to please him and gain his recognition, the father never acknowledged it.

On the other hand, some parents use **praise** in a manipulative way to get conformity. A child is good when he works the way you want, bad when he fails to conform. We bribe them with praise.

Punishment only proves that torture works—but only while you apply it. A "good child" who gets punished "unfairly" is confused. A "bad child" questions whether he is accepted. A child needs a sense of belonging. A discouraged child is a misbehaving child.

Pampering, or doing for the child what he can do for himself, is a basic put-down of the child and his abilities. It shows how strong the adult is and how weak and inadequate the child is.

Pitying, belittling, is another way to stress the superiority of the adult and the weakness, incompetence, inability of the child. Condescending remarks made to the child are in reality subtle insults.

In fact, all of the four P's of discipline reflect a superior to inferior relationship. They say, "Power makes right." The posture taken is one of moral and physical superiority. Mutual respect and cooperation are absent. Some examples:

Praise is used to reward compliance with orders.

Punishment is applied to force and enforce "cooperation."

Pampering is to do for others what they can do for themselves.

Pitying is to arrogantly point out the weaknesses of others.

All four P's of discipline invite serious abuses and problems:

Praise is not elevating, but evaluating. It bribes others.

Punishment is often not corrective, but hurtful and spiteful. It uses power and strength to get compliance.

Pampering is not mothering, but smothering; not parenting, but placating.

Pitying is not challenging, but crippling. It delights in assuming a superior, self-righteous, role. Contempt is conveyed.

Yes, we need discipline; but not the approach of the four P's. We need a method that shows mutual respect, positive regard, and a true willingness to cooperate with an equal. What do we teach by using the four P's? We teach power and control. Is it any wonder the big issue for children is freedom?

What would we *like* to teach? Freedom with responsibility! We can support the child in discovering the possibilities in life and seeing the choices available, then proceed to guide the child to discern the consequences that follow from their choices. We are free to make choices. We are also responsible for the results.

Bullies and bosses can make us do things we don't like. But that doesn't endear us to them. We want to cooperate with friendly people. We respond to those who encourage us as equals. We tend to avoid those who judge and treat us as inferior.

There is a big difference in attitude required for using expressions of either praise or encouragement. We could use words of praise to tell a famous conductor he did a good job. When he starts asking us specific questions about his performance, it would be wise to turn to words of encouragement. We could use words of encouragement when we simply want to tell him we enjoyed the performance. We are not critics; we are part of an appreciative audience.

When it comes to discipline, children have trained us well. We respond right on cue. Our main asset has been put on hold and we are too exhausted to use it. We have intelligence and experience, yet we hear ourselves saying, "I told you a thousand times not to do that." We are in a rut. We are reacting, not thinking and acting. Children do not waste their energy. Only adults do that.

Encouragement requires a new attitude. Instead of paying attention to what's wrong and what's going wrong, we must ignore or minimize the negative. Encouragement invites cooperation, not rebellion. It shows respect for the person. The encouragement process requires keeping our mouths shut when we are tempted to react to a child's misbehavior. It also means noticing and commenting on the positive, constructive behavior of the child. Encouragement is a basic form of human interaction. It respects efforts and struggles, not just the end results. It helps the other person find his or her own inner strength and value. It promotes peace and friendship by noticing the constructive contributions of others. It's a way of life, not just one more form of discipline.

Discipline.......Constriction

There is a need to respond appropriately and judicially with a firm "Yes" or "No" when it is required by our schedule, priorities, budgets, health, obligations, relationships and to all other areas of our lives. Doing it is the problem.

A wife complained to me about her husband. He was a very good man, but he had no time for his ten children and her. He complained that she didn't keep the house neat, when he found toys in the living room. He was VERY BUSY helping at the church, volunteering for the Rotary Club. He had no time for home except to eat and sleep. His priorities were wrong. He needed to make home the first priority. His work as the second priority and all else is last.

We need self-discipline as adults as much as children need discipline from parents. We must ration our time, energy and treasure in order to spend ourselves wisely. That effort requires some constriction, some pulling back and reorganizing.

We make New Year resolutions, we plan to do a Lenten sacrifice for others, intend to fight our addictions to drink, sex, gambling, food and whatever. We resolve, but then our good intention dissolve for lack of attention to our priorities and goals.

Hopefully we can have a good sense of humor about our human condition. We are, indeed, a work in progress. We can start again.

APPENDIX

I. A Brief Introduction to Adlerian Psychology

Adlerian psychology is based on the teachings of Alfred Adler, a contemporary of Freud. It is one of the few free-will psychologies practiced today. (Soft determinism allows for some influence upon the individual from heredity and environment, but the individual is considered more free than determined by them.) How do we use what nature and environment have given us? Use is stressed over possession.

Individual psychology is another name for Adler's theory of psychology. It stresses the uniqueness and unity of the human personality. It takes a holistic and phenomenological (subjective) approach to understanding the person.

Some major concepts in this approach include:

Self-Esteem

Each of us has a unique set of beliefs about ourselves, a map, so to speak, which guides us in approaching the basic tasks of life: work, friendship, love, self, and spiritual relationships. This basic image of ourselves is set around the age of six or eight.

Social Interest

Social interest, or *Geminschaftsgefuehl*, is an innate potentiality that needs to be consciously developed in a social context. It includes an empathetic identification with others for the common good, and an effort to resolve the major tasks of life, as well as striving toward the goal of belonging to an ideal cooperative community sub specie aeternitatis.

Value System

Adler's theory is based on certain attitudes. It stresses cooperation as equals, mutual respect, the need for everyone to be a contributor in society, and the need for balancing creative and constrictive behavior. This is an optimistic, educative, and preventive model of psychology. There is the belief that people can change. All of our behavior is ultimately purposeful. By discovering our goals, we can achieve a more significant sense of belonging and accept responsibility for the direction of our lives.

Counseling Approach

A socio-teleo-analytic approach is used in counseling.

socio- Since human beings are social in nature, there is a striving for belonging. This movement is idiographic, or subjectively unique to each individual. *Encouragement* is one of the major tools in assisting the individual to find his/her giftedness and inner value and worth. It helps the person find courage within themselves, unlike *praise*, which evaluates the individual according to external criteria and according to a superior–inferior relationship. Consideration of the social context and the attitudinal framework of the individual is important.

teleo- All behavior is purposeful. Whether it is eating, sleeping, drinking, sex, or whatever, it is done for a purpose. That purpose may be useful or useless in light of the common good. We want to understand the private logic of the individual, and his/her movement along the lines of that logic. In order to do that, we must discover what the person gets out of the behavior and what his or her goal is. This is a psychology of use, not possession. What the person does with what is possessed is more important than hereditary and environmental advantages or disadvantages.

Emotions are seen as sources of energy driving us to what we want to achieve. They can have negative or positive uses in reaching our goals in life.

analytic. An emphasis is placed on what the individual is aware of. Unconscious material is of value only when it emerges onto the awareness level. Thus dreams reveal anticipated problems and the rehearsing of possible solutions. Dreams gauge the emotional investment of energy in current problems.

Information about developmental factors in early childhood helps to explain present coping devices and the manner of approaching life and its tasks. The recording of early recollections and doing a Life Style analysis are Adlerian techniques that reveal a person's present attitudinal framework (biased apperception) and his/her interpretation of life in the here and now.

As hypotheses emerge concerning behavior and personality, these guesses will be shared with the client to ascertain their correctness. (This is called the stochastic method of counseling.) In this way the client begins to participate in, and take responsibility for, his/her own counseling progress.

The Adlerian Approach

Alfred Adler made an effort to follow common sense and to make his approach concrete and practical in the here and now. He avoided the reification of terms, although such terms as Life Style, social interest, self-esteem, and others have taken on specific meaning in the Adlerian system today. Childhood information is viewed as possible projections that relate more to the present than to the past. Present intentionality and purposefulness in behavior and movement pertain to the motivating goals of the individual. Thus goal setting and a treatment plan based on these goals is an essential aspect of Adlerian psychology. Progress in therapy will be gauged against these desired goals and objectives. Obviously, some adjustments and clarifications in stated goals can be expected with the possibility of concomitant discomfort for the client.

A sense of humor is considered an essential part of counseling. It is viewed as a sign of mental health and intelligence. It is seen as a tool for maintaining balance in life and managing stress.

Homework is an important part of the process and is viewed as an indicator of cooperation and a willingness to move in treatment.

ENCOURAGEMENT

Like the sense of humor, the ability to offer and receive encouragement requires training. A positive attitude of mind must be trained. Only then can we recognize opportunities for offering positive feedback. Without a conscious effort to perceive differently, we will typically focus on errors and mistakes in ourselves and others. We tend to judge from a goal of perfection and 100% accomplishment.

Golf is a great teacher of humility. We may strive to perfect our game rather than just play and enjoy it. I remember practicing a chip shot, an approach shot to the green. I kept at it until I could get eight out of ten balls into the cup. I felt a sense of accomplishment. I was ready to show my father what I could do. With him there, I got nine out of ten into the cup. His response was, "Forget the cup; look at your form; look at the swing you're using to hit the ball." Of course, the goal of the game is to get the ball into the cup with the fewest strokes. My father wanted that plus good form. Indeed, both of us wanted improvement.

It's hard to overlook the negative and go searching for the positive. We need to work for progress, not perfection and not just success and completion.

Perfectionists face a contradiction in their actions. They can get lost in fine details and in micromanaging and lose sight of the bigger picture.

The following quote from Cardinal Newman of England is a favorite motivator for me:

"Nothing would be done at all if a man waited till he could do it so well no one could find fault with it."

The goal of the en*courage*ment process is to develop courage in ourselves and in others. The focus is on strengths, a job well worked, constructive traits, assets, and anything we can build upon for further growth.

The wife of Dr. Rudolf Dreikurs wrote a book on art therapy titled *Purple Cows*. Cows can be many colors. If a child uses purple we can comment on the interesting choice of colors, or that he stayed within the lines, or worked very hard on it, etc. Somewhere there may be a purple cow, and now in fact there is!

It would be preferable that encouragement be a key ingredient in discipline by reinforcing positive behavior. For many parents, physical punishment isn't working. In a talk in which I suggested the use of encouragement instead of beatings and other physical punishments, a father stood up and challenged what I had been saying. I felt it was a breakthrough: he had been listening. I told him go ahead with it, but from experience it doesn't work. In fact, the teenager often takes up smoking, drinking, drugs, and running away. I had hit a nerve. His wife confirmed that all of those things were happening with their teenage son. Now they were ready to change **their** behavior with the hope it would benefit their son.

A misbehaving child is a discouraged child. If we accept this understanding of behavior, then we can do something about misconduct. First, we are alerted to possible traumatic incidents in the child's life, such as various types of abuse. Second, we are enabled to do something to help the child. We can deal with the precipitating cause. We can use encouragement. To punish a discouraged child is to invite rebellion and war.

It may seem easier and faster for parents to do everything for the child. It takes time and patience to teach and train a child. But new skills give confidence. For example, when a child is developmentally ready, he or she needs to be gently and patiently taught how to tie his/her shoes. Once the skill has been learned, practiced, and mastered, parents do a disservice by continuing to tie the child's shoes.

Pampering is doing for others what they can do for themselves. Codependency involves this same harmful doing for others. Encouragement supports trial and error learning. It goes beyond success and failure. Encouragement is life-giving and life-sharing. It is like the sun and water that makes the plants grow. Encouragement is essential to a well-balanced life. It gives hope, joy, and a belief in oneself and in others.

At times a child must be stopped and told a simple "No!" But most of the time we need the child's cooperation. Otherwise we become like police officers threatening dire consequences unless we are obeyed. We can be pleasant and friendly with children and not lose control.

Rudolf Dreikurs observed that discouraged children would prefer harsh words to being ignored. For him, goals explain actions. A child needs a sense of belonging and significance in the family and in society and will use whatever means are necessary to gain it. A child's behavior becomes less socially useful as his/her sense of worth is diminished. Since all behavior has a purpose, our intentions, our goals, are revealed by our actions. The misbehaving child is crying out for help. Dreikurs suggests four goals that the child may mistakenly think will bring significance: attention-getting, power, revenge, and assumed disability.

They are listed in descending order moving from constructive to destructive. Even though misconduct may seem destructive to the adult, to the child it may seem an effective way to get what he or she wants. A child would rather be punished than ignored.

The child who is a walking question mark becomes the rebel, then the mean, vicious bully, and finally gives up and quits trying. There is always a hidden, though mistaken, goal for all behavior. The child wants attention and mistakenly uses annoying means. The pampered child may feel controlled and strikes out in anger at the manipulation. An abused child may feel justified in returning the hurt in revenge. The shy child may retreat completely into silence. The more discouraged the child, the more desperate and destructive the behavior will become until he or she finally quits and gives up.

Behavior itself can indicate the level of discouragement and the goal. But our emotional reaction to challenging behavior may be a more certain way to recognize mistaken goals. Attention-getting will make us feel annoyed; stubbornness and power plays will anger us; spiteful and mean acts will hurt and enrage us; and finally, when the child quits, we will be tempted to give up as well. This last is obviously the most discouraging and greatest challenge to reverse.

If discouragement is the problem, the use of *en*couragement is a solution. There is a fine line between praise and encouragement. Praise looks to the end results; encouragement is a wider concept. Praise looks to specific successes; encouragement looks to lifelong achievements. A momentary success is fragile in comparison to achievements earned and won.

Again it helps to examine our emotional response to words of praise and encouragement in order to distinguish between them. Praise can make us slightly uncomfortable, embarrassed, and wondering if we really deserve it. Encouragement gives us joy and hope. Encouragement is simply commenting on what we are already doing and enjoying. It supports our ongoing efforts.

If we lose confidence in ourselves and our abilities, we become discouraged, and discouragement limits our hope. Our personal experiences may have biased us to focus on failures, mistakes, and on what is lacking and what has gone wrong. But success and achievement are the basis for growth and progress. Encouragement can provide the missing positive focus because it promotes creativity and a belief in unlimited possibilities. It fosters a spirit of hope and courage.

Experience taught us that the Berlin Wall would remain forever. It was a hopeless situation. But the wall is no longer. The human spirit has broken free. Each of us has our own walls. It is encouraging to recall that even the walls of Jericho fell—to joyful sounds and determined people. The encouragement process requires time and patience. It requires seeing the positive in others and overlooking their mistakes and weaknesses. It may mean doing things differently than our experience has taught us. The encouragement process is of pivotal importance in the life of a person. It may determine which side of life we select, crime or community service, despair or hope, war or peace. Encouragement allows us to speak with joy and live with courage.

II. Definitions of Humankind

Homo mechanicus: Man functioning as if part of a machine, a cog in the wheel.

Charlie Chaplin portrayed this concept of man in his movie *Modern Times*, in which he is caught up in a very large and consuming machine and is carried along imprisoned in its gears and rollers. The film reflects the loss of individuality and freedom during the period of the Industrial Revolution. He told critics that he merely followed an impulse to say something about men becoming standardized, turned into machines. He was accused of left-wing propaganda that fit the ideology of **communism**, but he just wanted to entertain.

Charles Dickens wrote about the inhumanity of child labor and the stagnation of a class society where everyone knows his place and is stuck there. In his novel *Dombey and Son*, he shows the arrogance of an **autocratic society** and the lack of empathy that can come from positions of wealth and power resulting in the suffering of their subjects.

Homo volens: The Psychology of Sigmund Freud and his theory of psychoanalysis placed an emphasis on feelings. Freud's work still has historical significance, but is not favored as a treatment today. He really didn't believe in change in an individual. He sought to help the person to adapt to his problem. If others didn't like or appreciate the person's behavior, then that was their problem: you do what you feel like doing.

We remember the hippies and the "love generation." The 1960s were a time for love and uninhibited relationships. "Free love" was in the air. **Anarchy** describes this understanding of humankind: do what you want—no responsibility, just freedom.

Homo sapiens: With space exploration and travel, with scientific breakthroughs in medicine and engineering, etc., we are in a phase of rational thinking. As we "conquer" nature, we seek a state of harmony with both nature and humankind. We seek equality and quality of life for all. We want fairness and justice for all. Hopefully these sentiments are found in **democracy.**

Homo ludens: The sense of humor, when applied to our daily routine and even to emergencies, should help us rise above the immediacy of our situation and see a bigger picture, a more unified view of people and life. Then our choice is not between success or failure, but among many options as to what should be done. This level establishes responsibility with freedom of choice, but strives to go further toward identifying with all humankind in altruistic and global goals. By seeking an enlightened sense of balance, and insight through growth in our sense of humor, we are working toward a transcendence of purpose and an empathy and compassion for all humankind. We are able to laugh at our clumsiness, our humanness, and seek to reduce the limits set upon us. We can challenge ourselves to expand our freedom with responsibility toward new areas of service and achievement for society. Rather than chemical highs, we gain natural highs.

Concluding question: NOW WHAT?

Will there be change, movement, challenge in our lives, or will it be more of the same?

Core belief necessary: **We must believe change is possible, no matter what!** We may not have a clear **goal** in mind, but we have the **means** by which we can start moving, i.e., **a sense of humor.**

Instead of expecting catastrophe or **success,** we can strive for progress, not perfection. Neither an idealized self nor a hopeless self serves us in achieving positive, creative movement in our lives.

Instead of thinking our choices are only between THIS and THAT, we need to expand our options to BOTH THIS **and** THAT. We have more options than we realize. Instead of a coin toss that gives us one side or the other, we can accept another point of view where the coin stands on edge offering both sides at once.

Instead of settling for the same old thing, we can gain a new vision, a new perspective on life and our situation.

Instead of expecting little of ourselves, we can discover we are unique and precious persons and gain a new sense of worth and value.

Ultimately, we need a strong sense of humor to survive with a sense of balance.

Summary

Homo mechanicus: autocratic—order without freedom
Homo volens: anarchy—freedom without order
Homo sapiens: democratic—freedom with order
Homo ludens: transcendent—beyond success and failure; creative

Autocratic: reward and punishment
    Superior/inferior (established roles)
    No need for structure, each knows his place
Volens: ruled by feelings and emotions
    Do as we please, uncontrolled
    Spoiled pampered brats
Sapiens: have judgment and responsibility
    The ability to think; we are responsible
    No system outside of people
    Each is motivated to achieve a goal.
    Purposeful and goal-directed.
    Sense of belonging
Ludens: leisure and higher contributions
    Transcendent and creative
    Virtue of *eutrapelia*
    Fulfilling life's tasks; relaxed
    Natural highs